a fresh look
how it works
why it matters

Liturgical worship

Mark Earey

Liturgical worship

a fresh look
how it works
why it matters

worship

Mark Earey

CHURCH HOUSE
PUBLISHING

Church House Publishing
Church House
Great Smith Street
London SW1P 3NZ

ISBN 0 7151 2081 6

Published 2002 by Church House Publishing
Second impression 2005

Typeset in Frutiger 9pt

Printed by Biddles Ltd, King's Lynn.

Contents

Acknowledgements

I would like to thank the many people who have read and commented on an earlier draft of this material: Margaret Dye, Anne Wood, Kathy Robertson, Jill Perrett, Tony Perrett, Paul Bradshaw, Gilly Myers, Phil Steer, Alison Earey and Charles Prest. They have all, in different ways, encouraged me in the work and contributed to the final version, though, of course, they have no responsibility for the weaknesses that remain. John and Dianne Law provided hospitality at a crucial point, and I am grateful to them also.

The book is dedicated, with grateful thanks, to Colin J. D. Greene and P. Mark Pullinger, who between them brought liturgical worship to life for me.

Copyright acknowledgements

The publisher gratefully acknowledges permission to reproduce copyright material in this publication. Every effort has been made to trace and contact copyright holders. If there are any inadvertent omissions we apologize to those concerned and will ensure that a suitable acknowledgement is made at the next reprint.

Scripture quotations from *New Revised Standard Version of the Bible* copyright © 1989 Division of Christian Education of the National Council of Churches in the USA. Used by permission. All rights reserved.

Anglican Church in Aotearoa, New Zealand and Polynesia: Extract from *A New Zealand Prayer Book*, 1989. Reproduced by permission (p. 79).

The Archbishops' Council: Extracts from *Common Worship: Services and Prayers for the Church of England*, 2000. Reproduced by permission (pp. 10, 66, 76, 78-9, 81).

Kingsway Publications: Extract from Graham Kendrick, *Worship*, Kingsway Publications, 1984 (p. 10)

Methodist Publishing House: Extract from *Let the People Worship: Report of the Commission on Worship*, 1988 (p. 10) and *Methodist Worship Book*, 1999 (p. 76). Copyright © Trustees for Methodist Church Purposes. Used by permission.

Church of Scotland, Panel on Worship: Extract from *Common Order*, First Order for Evening Service (p. 79).

Introduction

This book has been written for a number of different sorts of people. First, it is for those who want, or need, to discover and understand liturgical worship for the first time. It is also for those who already know and love liturgy, but who want to step back and take a fresh look at it. It may also be of use to those whose experience or perception of liturgical worship has not been good, but who are determined to discover what it can be at its best, rather than dwelling on what it has been at its worst.

I have written from a belief that liturgy takes us to the very heart of what it is to be a Christian and live in the gap between the 'now' and the coming kingdom. Therefore, although questions about where particular elements or forms of liturgy come from can be fascinating and are important (and there is some of that here), what liturgy does to us is altogether more significant, and that is where this book focuses.

I must also stress that this is not a book about *the* liturgy. Though it includes examples from actual liturgies (mainly from the Church of England, simply because these are the forms of service that I know best), it does not seek to persuade the reader that there is only one right way of worshipping God. I do not believe that the liturgical patterns of one Church or denomination are inherently superior to those of another. A form of service is no more above criticism than a hymn or song.

This book seeks to look beyond the common outward accompaniments of particular liturgies from particular traditions – the words spoken, the actions performed, and the books that are sometimes used – to consider how liturgy, more generally, works. I have written it to help people who are not, and who do not expect to become, liturgy specialists, but who want or need to get a feel for liturgy and some basic 'rules of the game'. My hope is that, armed with this understanding, those who lead and plan worship will approach the task with renewed vision and confidence.

The book contains some history, but it is not primarily a book about the history of liturgy. Some may find its broad-brush approach frustrating, but the detailed history of dates, names and places, and the particular manifestations of liturgical worship in different traditions and at different times, are well covered elsewhere, and I have given an indication of where to turn for further information in the Appendix.

In the first two chapters we look at Christian worship generally and liturgy in particular and consider the relationship between the two. Chapters 3 and 4 delve into some of the history. I have not attempted to chart the history of every sort of Christian worship from baptism to burial. Instead, I have given a general overview (Chapter 3), followed by a more specific focus on the Eucharist (Chapter 4). I have taken this approach for two reasons: first, there is not room in a book this size to consider the history and elements of every sort of Christian worship; and, second, the Eucharist has been an important part of Christian worship for most Christians during most of the history of the Christian Church, and is likely to be of more interest than any other specific form of worship.

Chapters 5 and 6 look at some of the different ways that liturgy gives shape to our way of seeing the world, understanding our lives, and worshipping and experiencing God.

Chapters 7 and 8 come closest to looking at particular forms of liturgy and I have saved them until last because of that; I wanted to establish the principles first. In Chapters 7 and 8 I have taken a similar approach to that of Chapters 3 and 4, looking first at elements of liturgical worship in general and then looking at elements particular to the Eucharist.

Each chapter concludes with some points 'For further reflection...'. These are in the form of questions that could be addressed either individually or in a small group. They are not 'study questions', but are intended to help readers to tease out the practical implications of the book and connect it with their own experience of worship. If you find them an annoying interruption rather than a help, skip them.

There is an old joke whose punchline suggests that you are more likely to be able to negotiate with a terrorist than with a liturgist. This book's message is that there is little (if anything) that is non-negotiable in the practice of liturgical worship – but there is a huge amount which, renewed and reinterpreted in every generation, takes us to the heart of the Christian faith.

1

What is Christian worship?

Though this book is specifically about liturgical worship, we begin
with a look at the broader question of what Christian worship, more
generally, is all about. Only by understanding that bigger picture can
we properly 'get in close' to see the particular contribution that
liturgical worship can make in the life of the Church.

Worship and life

Christians have a problem when they talk about worship. On the
one hand, they use the term as shorthand for the sort of activities
that they commonly engage in when they meet together, normally
but not exclusively, on a Sunday: singing, praying, reading from the
Bible and responding to its message, remembering Jesus with bread
and wine.

On the other hand, we know from both the Old Testament prophets
and the New Testament that, for Christians, worship can never be
reduced to these ritual words and actions; it is about the whole of
life and how we live it.

Consider this, from the Old Testament:

> *Take away from me the noise of your songs;*
> *I will not listen to the melody of your harps.*
> *But let justice roll down like waters,*
> *and righteousness like an everflowing stream.*

Amos 5.23-24

Turning to the New Testament, consider, for instance, what the
apostle Paul writes:

> *I appeal to you therefore, brothers and sisters, by the mercies*
> *of God, to present your bodies as a living sacrifice, holy and*
> *acceptable to God, which is your spiritual worship.*

Romans 12.1

It is worth dwelling on Paul's summary of what spiritual (or, in some translations, 'reasonable') worship involves. Note especially that he writes about 'bodies'. He could just as easily have written, 'Offer your spirits [or 'souls'] as a living sacrifice', but he chose not to. There is no room here for the idea that worship is primarily in the head or the heart; Christian worship, acceptable to God, is to be nothing less than the offering of our whole selves (and note the corporate emphasis – *our* bodies offered make a living sacrifice). Paul makes this clear in the way that he continues in the rest of Romans 12. The chapter is full of the practical issues of daily life which follow on from this 'spiritual worship':

- being transformed in our thinking and ordering our relationships and lifestyles accordingly (vv. 2, 9-11);

- having a realistic assessment of ourselves (vv. 3,16);

- using our gifts to serve others (vv. 6-8);

- having patience in suffering (v. 12);

- putting others first (v. 10);

- offering hospitality (v. 13);

- seeking to reconcile those in dispute (vv. 16,18);

- blessing those who make life difficult for us and not taking revenge (vv. 14,17-21).

Paul takes the concept of sacrifice, familiar to his readers, and gives it a new twist. The sacrifice he is writing about is not a religious ritual performed by a special caste of persons on behalf of the community at a religious time and in a religious place. His idea is that sacrifice is for everyone, everyday, in every activity. Worship is doing good, caring for the most vulnerable and seeking justice for the oppressed (cf. Isaiah 1.10-17 and Amos 5.21-24).

This radical, thoroughgoing approach to worship was reflected in the patterns and structures of the life of the early Church. It caused the first followers of Jesus to be looked on with great suspicion in the Roman empire. They were seen as 'atheists' because their 'religion' was strangely lacking in those things which were regarded as constituting proper worship: sacrifices, priests and temples. These were missing from the new religion because Christians recognized that Jesus had fulfilled these things in his own person.

- They saw that the ultimate sacrifice was now the life of Jesus himself, freely laid down for others (Hebrews 9.11-14, 24-28).

- What is more, Jesus was not only the sacrifice, he was also the priest who offered the sacrifice (Hebrews 9.11).

- This meant that there was no need for a temple, or for any other sort of special building in which to focus the sense of God's presence, for Christians saw that if you wanted to look for God, the 'place' was a person: Jesus himself. As John wrote, 'The Word became flesh and lived among us' (John 1.14). Paul put it like this: 'In [Christ] all the fullness of God was pleased to dwell' (Colossians 1.19 and 2.9).

These things – sacrifice, priesthood and temple – find a further fulfilment in Christ's body, the Church:

- Christians, like Jesus, are to lay down their lives. The call to 'take up the cross and follow Jesus' was a call to live as those condemned to death (Mark 8.34). Peter writes that they are to offer 'spiritual sacrifices, acceptable to God' (1 Peter 2.5) and Paul, as we have seen, calls on them to offer themselves to God as a living sacrifice (Romans 12.1).

- They are also to see themselves as a 'royal priesthood' (1 Peter 2.5, 9).

- Christians are corporately and individually described as 'temples' of the Holy Spirit and living temples (1 Corinthians 6.19 and 1 Peter 2.5).

Sunday matters

This is not to say, however, that special and symbolic words and actions, performed when Christians gather together, are no longer of any value at all. The Old Testament prophets criticized Israel's worship primarily because of a lack of integrity between corporate worship and the rest of life, rather than because the rituals and prayers themselves were wrong. Though the Church had no need of its own priests, sacrifices and temples (in the former, Jewish, sense), there is lots of evidence within the New Testament of Christians meeting together, and some clues as to what they did.

- Acts 2 records them meeting in homes and in the temple (meaning the outer courts where Jews were accustomed to meet and pray, especially at the times when sacrifices were going on inside). It mentions the apostles' teaching, fellowship, the breaking of bread, praising God, support of the poor, and prayers (Acts 2.42-47).

- In 1 Corinthians 11 Paul gives instructions about how to celebrate what he calls 'the Lord's Supper'.

- In 1 Corinthians 14 Paul lists 'a hymn, a lesson, a revelation, a tongue, or an interpretation' as the elements which believers might bring and offer to the gathering (v. 26). He also gives instructions about the use of speaking in tongues in the meeting, with particular attention to the impact this would have on any visitors.

- Ephesians 5.18-20 and Colossians 3.16-17 both mention, 'psalms, hymns, and spiritual songs'.

- Accounts of the worship of heaven are given in the book of Revelation. These may have reflected or influenced the worship of the Churches on earth (see, for instance, Revelation 4.1-11; 5.11-14; 7.1-17).

- The 'songs' recorded in Luke's Gospel may have reflected what happened in Christian worship and also influenced it. See for instance the songs of Mary (sometimes called the 'Magnificat', from the first line of the Latin version: Luke 1.46-55), Zechariah (sometimes called the 'Benedictus': Luke 1.68-79) and Simeon (sometimes called the 'Nunc Dimittis': Luke 2.28-32).

- Words and phrases used in corporate worship were passed on in their Aramaic form, even when used by Greek-speaking people (e.g. 'Amen', 'Abba', 'Hallelujah', 'Maranatha').

- Other forms of prayer, praise and blessing, and statements of belief, appear to be in a rhythmic form, suggesting that they were known and often repeated, perhaps in worship (e.g. Romans 10.9 and 11.33-36; 1 Corinthians 8.6 and 15.3-5; Ephesians 5.14; 1 Timothy 1.17, 3.16).

- Hints survive of gestures or actions, such as kneeling to pray, the sharing of the 'holy kiss', and raising hands in prayer (Acts 21.5; 1 Corinthians 16.20; 1 Timothy 2.8).

Hence, when Christians talk about worship, they have to bear in mind both the big picture of *Worship* (with, as it were, a capital letter) in its broadest and truest sense of living life for God, *and* its corporate expression when the Church gathers for *worship* (with a small 'w'). This latter worship is what we might call symbolic or representative worship, in that it focuses and points towards the bigger Worship. What is vital is that the two never become disconnected in such a way that worship becomes an escape from life, rather than part of life.

The list of clues from the New Testament, given above, includes descriptions of what the first Christians did, some forms of words that may have been used, instructions to particular congregations, and general indications of content. It includes three dimensions:

- elements of human-to-human relationships (fellowship, supporting the poor, statements of common belief, sharing a 'holy kiss');

- the God-to-human dimension (listening to Scripture, receiving teaching, a tongue or a revelation);

- the human-to-God dimension (praising God, singing hymns, praying).

What is missing, however, is systematic *prescriptive* teaching about what the Church's corporate worship should include – teaching that could guide us today. This is one of the reasons why worship can be a very contentious issue for Christians. We may not be looking for detailed instructions about sacrifices, but for most of us what we do on Sunday is very significant for sustaining us in our faith during the rest of the week. We know that the Church's corporate worship *matters* and we have a strong desire to 'get it right': to please God and strengthen the congregation to serve him.

If only we had some clear, direct teaching from Jesus himself – something like this:

> And Jesus went up onto a hill and taught them, saying, 'When you go to church make sure that the service starts between 10 and 11 o'clock in the morning and ends after no more than an hour (preferably with coffee or other refreshments). And when you worship, always start with a formal greeting before the first hymn. After the hymn, kneel down and confess your sins to God, using these or other authorized forms of words...

When you consider how much energy and time is devoted to preparing, leading and taking part in acts of worship in churches around the world every week it is amazing just how little instruction we have from Jesus about what we should do.

What little we do have includes the following:

The Lord's Prayer

When teaching his disciples about prayer, Jesus said, 'When you pray, say: "Father…"' (Luke 11.2) or 'Pray then in this way: Our Father…"' (Matthew 6.9). We don't know for sure whether he intended us to use exactly the same words every time and, indeed, we don't *have* the exact words, for this prayer is recorded twice in the New Testament in two slightly different forms and in two different contexts:

- In Matthew's Gospel it is part of Jesus' more general teaching on prayer as part of his 'Sermon on the Mount';

- In Luke's Gospel it is given in response to the disciples' direct request to be taught how to pray, after they have watched Jesus himself at prayer.

On top of that, each of these recorded versions is a translation into Greek from the Aramaic (a form of Hebrew) in which Jesus presumably taught the prayer. We, in turn, have various English translations (some in modern and some in traditional language) from those Greek versions. No wonder the Church still has such arguments over which form of the Lord's Prayer to use (see also Chapter 7, page 85). However, it is worth noting that what we do have here is evidence of Jesus teaching a short, easily memorable pattern of prayer – and one that assumes a corporate context ('Our Father', not, 'My Father').

Holy Communion

Here, again, it is tempting to think that we have more information than we do. The command, 'Do this in remembrance of me' (Luke 22.19), is recorded, but there is no indication of *when* to do it – simply, 'Do this, as often as you drink it' (1 Corinthians 11.25). Nor did Jesus tell us *how* to do it or what to *say*. We don't know that he intended it to be a public ritual taking place regularly (see Chapter 4). In fact, one could argue that there is just as much evidence to suggest that footwashing should be a regular part of our worship – perhaps weekly or even daily – for Jesus said, after washing his disciples' feet at the Last Supper, 'So if I, your Lord and Teacher, have washed your feet, you also ought to wash one another's feet. For I have set you an example, that you also should do as I have done to you' (John 13.14-15).

Jesus' teaching about worship

Ironically, the one time when Jesus did directly address the issue of worship, it was almost by accident, in response to a passing comment by a Samaritan woman. Jesus' fascinating discussion with the woman at the well concludes with his radical vision of the worship God requires:

> *'Woman, believe me, the hour is coming when you will worship the Father neither on this mountain [Gerizim] nor in Jerusalem . . . the hour is coming, and is now here, when the true worshippers will worship the Father in spirit and truth, for the Father seeks such as these to worship him. God is spirit, and those who worship him must worship in spirit and truth.'*
>
> John 4.21-24

Interestingly, this conversation does not reflect the experience of two nations worshipping different gods, but people who worshipped the same God, but couldn't agree on how (or where) that one God preferred to be worshipped – a disagreement that is not so very far from the disagreements within Christian churches today about styles and patterns of worship.

Jesus seems to be wanting to lift the woman's sights beyond the arguments to something bigger. The gist of what he says to her seems to be that you can't put God in a box, pinning him down to this mountain or that mountain, this temple or that. So far, so good. But what does he mean by worship 'in spirit and truth'? In John's Gospel the Spirit is associated with unpredictability: 'The wind blows where it chooses, and you hear the sound of it, but you do not know where it comes from or where it goes. So it is with everyone who is born of the Spirit' (John 3.8). But the Spirit is also associated with the truth: 'I will ask the Father, and he will give you another Advocate, to be with you for ever. This is the Spirit of truth' (John 14.16-17); 'When the Spirit of truth comes, he will guide you into all the truth' (John

16.13). Jesus also associated *himself* with the truth: 'I am the way, and the truth, and the life' (John 14.6). He also described the truth as something that liberates: 'If you continue in my word, you are truly my disciples; and you will know the truth, and the truth will make you free' (John 8.31-32). Spirit and truth are not two separate things, but two interrelated and interdependent things – maybe even two ways of saying the same thing.

Perhaps what we have here is something to do with integrity. The true worshippers will worship in ways that are true to themselves and true to the God in whom they believe. Those ways may vary from place to place and time to time (for God cannot be put in a box), but the God who is worshipped will remain the same.

If this is right, then Jesus' teaching reinforces the message of the Old Testament prophets. Corporate worship should engage, in a representative way, with things that matter in our daily lives: hospitality, listening to God, community, sharing the good news, serving our neighbour. This connection is not simply one-way (with worship reflecting life); nor is it an empty symbol. Because it is engagement with the living God, corporate worship, with its symbolic and representative nature, has the potential and the power to be formative; it can shape our lives in Christ and our understanding (including our unspoken assumptions) about God.

The formative nature of public worship

Take a simple question: 'Why do we read the Bible in church?' Here are two possible answers:

- so that the members of the congregation will engage with at least one passage of the Bible this week;

- because it gives the preacher a peg on which to hang a sermon.

These are good reasons and both are true, but they are not the end of the answer. Christians read the Bible in church because the Bible is vital to the Christian life. We read it publicly because of how important it is for the whole of the week, not just because it is important on Sunday. The very fact that it is read, week in, week out, irrespective of whether we feel like it or not, is shaping our expectations about the importance of the Bible to Christians.

What about the prayers? Sometimes it feels like little more than reeling off a shopping list to God, even when they are led well. But the main reason for praying publicly and corporately for the world, the Church, our communities and those in need is to give shape to the fact that God is concerned about those things all the time and that we are called to share that concern. Prayer without matching action during the rest of the week is hollow: but prayer shapes our action as well as reflecting it.

This 'reminding' and 'shaping' is not something of which we are conscious – but over a period of years it forms our hidden assumptions.

Case Study: How worship forms us as Christians

Lucy was brought up as a regular worshipper in an Anglican church. When she left school and went to university she began attending an independent church, which deliberately avoided any conscious liturgical structure for its worship. The services were always lively and enjoyable and the sermons challenging – yet there always seemed to be something missing. After several months she realized what it was: what her home church called the 'Prayers of Intercession'. At her new church they often confessed their failings to God (in prayer or song) and frequently prayed for help in sharing their faith. But in four months they had never prayed publicly for the government, or for those who were sick, bereaved, or in need.Those things came up now and again if the sermon happened to lean that way, but there was no sense of regularly bringing them before God. And she only noticed that it was missing because for years and years she had belonged to a church in which the intercessions were part of the liturgical structure. If she was honest, Lucy had to admit that she often found the intercessions one of the most boring parts of the service, but, boring or not, they had made a difference to her understanding of what corporate worship was all about. What is more, she realized that her passionate concern for justice in the world (about which she was often teased by her friends) had come, not from sermons, but from years of exposure to public prayer for the poor and oppressed.

In the short term it matters enormously that everything we do in church is done as well as possible – and week after week of dull and uninspiring intercessions can be a big turn off. But maybe, in the long term, what matters even more is whether certain things happen, or don't happen, at all. Corporate worship forms our assumptions by what it symbolizes. What is missing matters as much as what is present.

In Chapter 2 we will argue that the two-way connection between corporate worship and living the Christian life matters so much that it should not be left to chance, and that liturgy is a structured way of making sure that this connection is made.

For further reflection...

1. Look at these statements about worship. What strengths and weaknesses can you identify in each of them?

> *Central to our worship is the proclamation of the one, perfect self-offering of the Son to the Father.*
>
> *Worship not only strengthens Christian for witness and service, but is itself a forum in which Christ is made known.*
>
> *. . . worship itself is a pilgrimage – a journey into the heart of the love of God.*
>
> Preface, Common Worship, *Church of England forms of worship, 2000*

> *Worship is God's enjoyment of us and our enjoyment of him.*
>
> Graham Kendrick, Worship, *1984*

> *At heart, worship is a statement of faith. We worship because we believe in a certain kind of God.*
>
> Let the People Worship, *Methodist report, 1988*

2. Can you now make a simple definition which sums up your understanding of worship?

3. Look again at your definition. Is it a definition of worship in general or of specifically Christian worship? What is it that makes worship 'Christian'?

4. How conscious are you that your activities from Monday to Saturday, outside church meetings, are 'worship'?

5. In what ways does your church's corporate worship reflect God's concerns for justice, peace and integrity in daily living? What could you do to increase that sense of connection between life and corporate worship?

2

What is 'liturgy'?

Most Christians, of whatever Church and tradition, are comfortable with the word 'worship'. The word 'liturgy', however, is not so universally used or understood. To some it feels more obscure, more technical, only for 'that sort of Christian'. I spent years avoiding the term, always preferring what I saw as the more straightforward term 'worship'.

Liturgy is a technical term and, though technical terms can be off-putting, they do act as a concise way of making meaning more precise.

■ As we saw in Chapter 1, Christian 'worship' means both living our lives for God and gathering as God's people with a focus on God.

  'Liturgy' is always about the corporate gathering.

■ 'Worship' can also cover private devotions or singing along to a praise tape on your own in the car.

  'Liturgy' is always bigger than the personal, even though it may encompass it.

■ Within the corporate gathering, 'worship' can be used in different ways. It can mean the whole service (as on the notice board which proclaims, 'Divine Worship at 11.00am') and it can also be used in more limited ways to refer particularly to the human-to-God dimension (as in, 'Let's worship God') or to particular aspects of that worship (as in, 'We'll now have a time of worship', meaning, 'We're going to sing some songs').

  'Liturgy' always encompasses the whole service with its three dimensions: human-to-human; God-to-human; human-to-God.

There is worship which is liturgical and there is worship which is not: the two terms are not straight alternatives, even though their meanings overlap.

Understanding the word

Put simply, 'liturgy' is the term that the Church adopted to describe what we would call a 'church service'.

It comes from a Greek word and means literally 'public works'. In the Roman world, outside the Church, it described the duty of citizens to engage in good works of benefit to the community, including religious rites performed for the public good. In common usage it came to mean any service done for someone else. In the Greek translation of the Old Testament (often called the Septuagint) the word was used for the service of the priests and Levites in doing their specifically religious 'work'. When the Church began to draw parallels between Christian leaders and the priests of the Old Testament, the word was taken from its Old Testament context and attached to Christian gatherings for worship, especially to the Eucharist.

However, the New Testament is clear that the body of Christ is a Church *of* priests, rather than a Church *with* priests. That meant that the term 'liturgy' could not be attached only to the work of the ordained leaders: in the Church *everyone* has work to do for God and others, both in the world and in corporate worship. The earlier use of liturgy to mean 'service to others' surfaced again – our corporate worship serves God, one another and the world. Within it we each have a 'liturgy', a part to play for the good of the whole rather than our personal benefit.

Is your church 'liturgical'?

Though liturgy can be a useful technical term, its primary meaning can be clouded by association with secondary elements.

Imagine that a friend has invited you to go to church with her on Sunday. You ask casually what sort of service it will be. 'Oh, we're fairly liturgical,' she says. What image does that conjure up? You might be expecting some or all of the following:

- books (or printed orders of service in card or booklet form);
- some form of special clothes for the leader;
- words for the congregation to join in saying or singing (in addition to songs or hymns);
- some sort of special title for the day (such as 'Third Sunday of Epiphany');

- a building or worship space which seems to be full of clearly symbolic furniture and may be elaborate or highly decorated;

- the use of symbolic actions and objects, such as formal processions, lighted candles or the burning of incense.

It's no wonder that we often think of liturgy as a 'style' of worship. Other things being equal, we expect it to be towards the more formal end of the spectrum, perhaps a bit 'churchy' in its language, and fairly elaborate in its ceremonies and the decor of the building. But liturgy is much more than a matter of style.

Words

Sometimes 'liturgy' is used to mean the spoken words in the service, as opposed to the songs or hymns. When Spring Harvest started printing Bible passages and prayers interspersed with the songs in their songbook, they at first called them 'Words for Worship' and 'spoken responses'. Later they started calling them 'Prayers and Liturgy' – where 'liturgy' meant sets of words that included congregational responses, as distinguished from the songs. In casual usage in churches, this is often what is meant by 'liturgy'.

Even in churches where some 'liturgical texts' (such as the Gloria in Excelsis or a eucharistic prayer) are *sung*, people sometimes talk about 'the liturgy' when they mean the words in the service book, to distinguish them from words that are in the hymn-book.

But liturgy is bigger than words: it encompasses what we do in the service as well as what we say. To use technical language, liturgy is 'rite': a pattern of words and actions that have meaning for a community – like lighting the candles on a birthday cake and singing 'Happy Birthday'. It includes silence, movement, posture, symbol. It engages us as whole persons: body, mind and spirit.

Books

The false idea that liturgy is primarily about words leads us to expect to find liturgy in books – and often the connection is drawn so strongly that we imagine that liturgy is inherently connected with the use of books or some other printed form of service.

In fact books and orders of service were fairly late arrivals on the liturgical scene. Books only became used for worship when the services got complicated and the leaders needed to know what to say. These books were hand-copied and only for the leaders. The people had no books – they knew their parts by heart.

At the time of the sixteenth-century Reformation the recent invention of moveable type allowed the Reformers to use printing to spread their ideas and to change worship. In the Church of England, printing enabled Archbishop Thomas Cranmer to enforce a changed liturgy literally overnight.

Print was also used by the Roman Catholic Church. In the medieval period, local churches copied the way things were done in prestigious centres. In England the most common version of the Catholic Mass was the 'use' (i.e. the form of service) of Sarum (i.e. Salisbury cathedral). Hand-copied service books for the priest were expensive and so were only rarely replaced. This meant that the liturgy evolved at a slow pace, with strong family likenesses but differences in the detail from one place to another. After the Council of Trent (1545-62) the Roman Catholic liturgy was standardized much more, again through the use of printing.

The printed word lends itself to liturgical forms of worship because of its inherent stability. Writing liturgy down (both words and instructions) can simply be a way of passing it on. It has been used as a means of bringing rapid change to forms of worship, but it can also be used as a way of making liturgy very resistant to change. Either way, liturgy itself is not dependent on the printed word, any more than singing is dependent on hymn-books.

Print and flexibility in liturgy

Modern technology now allows us to use print but to vary the content according to the time of year or the needs of a particular congregation. The Church of England's *Common Worship* services were available in electronic form (including via the Internet) at the same time as they came out in book form. *The Methodist Worship Book* is also available electronically and many other denominations around the world put liturgical resources on the Internet. This enables even those congregations which are part of consciously 'liturgical' churches to produce their own orders of service tailored to their particular circumstances.

Overhead projection and data projectors are allowing some churches to use liturgical texts without any printed material at all – and that makes it even easier to use liturgical texts and structures flexibly, making last minute changes but still allowing for the congregation to have a part.

Fixity

If you put together the (false) idea that liturgy is primarily about words with the fact that those words are printed in books, the idea soon develops that liturgy is about fixity, stability and a lack of flexibility or spontaneity. For instance, when the Church of England began the process of introducing new forms of service (*Common Worship*) a common question asked by ordinary worshippers was, 'Why are they changing the services again?' The question revealed an assumption: that the natural state for liturgy was fixity and stability. Change was seen as an interruption to, rather than a natural element in, liturgical worship. The question should be the other way round: 'Why should the service stay the same?' Forms of liturgy originated simply as patterns of word and action that were shared between churches. Good practice and bright ideas were copied and passed around.

Liturgical worship has, historically, tended to remain fairly constant, to include standard elements and to repeat ritual actions and familiar words. But this is not confined to 'liturgical' churches: even churches that pride themselves on their freedom in worship tend to settle down into a regular pattern, and churches whose worship is dominated by hymns or worship songs will have a basic (if evolving) repertoire.

Liturgy is not conservative or resistant to change for deep theological reasons, but simply because *any* complex activity involving lots of people in different roles will tend to resist change if it is to continue to allow for participation by those present. For instance, the audience at a pantomime is only able to get involved and play its part if the script and the cast stick to the expected pattern. A decent round of 'Oh yes he did! – Oh no he didn't!' requires that people know the words and understand the right context in which to use them. If the cast don't give the right visual and verbal clues the audience won't know what to do. Change can come – but it won't happen overnight because it needs to take everyone with it. Incidentally, note that at the pantomime no one in the audience needs to have their words printed out. Like most rituals, we learn our part by participating with others who have been there before. Ritual (like the Christian faith itself) is passed on, not learnt from a book.

Liturgical worship often incorporates elements that seem archaic (words, ceremonies, clothes, etc.). This is simply because things that are 'passed on', even if they are still valuable today, often carry with them the signs that they originated in a different era. This should, however, never be allowed to develop into the idea that archaic things are intrinsically 'better' or more holy.

Liturgy in the East

In the Eastern (or 'Orthodox') Churches, 'liturgy' is used in a slightly different way. 'The Liturgy' always means the Eucharist. In that tradition 'liturgy' is assumed to be, in essence, unvarying and stable over time and from place to place.

Getting to the heart of the meaning

So liturgy is not about worship in a certain 'style'; it's not primarily about words or books; neither is it about forms of service that are unalterable or inherently archaic. At the heart of liturgy is an understanding of public worship that goes beyond the personal encounter with God (without denying it) to the corporate drama of being the people of God.

The Christian way of life is itself a drama. In it, we take on a new role that God has given us. It involves 'playing the part' of those who are newborn by the Spirit, holy and loving, even while we know that we fail to fulfil this role in many ways. This is not some sort of 'play-acting' or pretending. God calls us to grow into these roles as we grow as Christians. By his Spirit he transforms us into the likeness of Christ. But this side of heaven, there is always that tension between the person I am and the person God is making me. It is like the tension in an actor between the actor's natural self and the part that he or she is playing. To play the part you have to understand both the points of contact and the contradictions between your natural self and the character in the play. If you play the part for long enough, the part influences you as much as you influence the part.

Liturgy is the rehearsal – the many rehearsals – for the parts we are called to take both in the world now and in eternity with God. We each have a part to play in God's work in the world, and liturgy reflects this, but our personal engagement with God at an individual level finds its proper place within the 'duty and joy' of the corporate event.

Hence, some worship may call itself 'liturgical', but if it turns us in on our own worshipping experience, fails to connect us with the bigger picture, or robs us of our part, it is not liturgy. Conversely, public worship which does not claim the title 'liturgy' but draws us into the drama, allows us to play our part and shapes us for life in Christ, can be true liturgy: the work of the people, for the people.

What should we expect from liturgy?

We have already seen that all corporate worship (whether you call it liturgy or not) has a powerful representative and symbolic aspect, which can shape our faith and our lives. What, then, are the core values and particular emphases of worship that is deliberately liturgical?

Liturgical worship is deliberately and consciously:

- **clearly structured**, rather than 'accidentally' structured or deliberately unstructured;

- **essentially corporate**, rather than focused on the individual's experience or local preferences;

- **richly holistic**, rather than focused on the mind alone or words alone.

Of course, this is not a description of liturgical worship as you may have experienced it: this is a summary of what liturgical worship, at its best, ought to be about. And any of these emphases may, naturally, be present in other forms of worship; true liturgical worship simply tries deliberately to hold them together.

Clearly structured

Perhaps the most obvious thing about liturgical worship is that it has a conscious structure (which has been determined, at least in part, before the service begins and by the wider Church beyond the local congregation). In fact, all worship has a structure; liturgical worship simply gives attention to this structure in a deliberate way and with an eye to the long-term, as well as the short-term, implications.

Structure which is fixed in some way can become a prison, though it can also be thought of as a skeleton (or even a safety net). Though liturgical worship often does mean that the service is followed in much the same way each week, it needn't be like that. There is nothing inherent in liturgy that means there can be no room for the spontaneous, creative, 'Spirit-led', or extemporary. The liturgy provides a norm – a 'default' setting – to be followed unless there is a strong sense of the need to divert from it or add to it. It is founded on the belief that the Spirit of God works just as much through advance planning as through spontaneous changes; and just as much through the wider Church as through the views of a local leader.

Isn't liturgy just 'vain repetition'?

> When you are praying, do not heap up empty phrases [or 'use not vain repetitions' as the Authorized Version puts it] as the Gentiles do; for they think that they will be heard because of their many words.
>
> Matthew 6.7

Some people worry that liturgy will descend into the 'vain repetition' that Jesus criticized. It can, of course – but so can using the same song or hymn more than once. What Jesus criticized was *vain* repetition – piling up the words, thinking that God is more likely to listen – not repetition as such. Though liturgical worship tends to repeat at least some of the same words and actions week by week, it avoids the repetition within one service, or even within one prayer, which so easily results if there is no structure and shape to worship. Liturgy can therefore be a way of avoiding repetition – especially if the Christian year is used to bring out different emphases at different times of the year.

On the other hand, a 'spontaneous' prayer which covers much the same ground each week could feel pretty repetitive…

At its most profound, liturgy is about bringing (or reflecting) God's order in a disordered world – an order that echoes the work of the Spirit brooding over the waters at the dawn of creation. Like the work of creation, it should never be static or leave us unmoved and unchanged. Liturgy should draw us inexorably into the eternal, creative, freedom-bringing order of the kingdom of heaven.

Essentially corporate

Liturgy always has a corporate aspect. How I praise God at home in my own prayers is between me and God. When I join with the Church, however, I am part of something bigger. I don't simply bring my private worship and put it together with the personal worship of others, like eggs that happen to be in the same eggbox. Liturgy is more like an omelette: eggs are broken and something new results. No wonder public worship is sometimes hard! It involves being broken in order to be remade, because it means balancing my preferences with the needs of others, perhaps even sacrificing my preferences. We worship *in* Christ, as part of the body.

Liturgical worship is also deliberately corporate in the sense that it belongs to all of us, not just to the leader. That limits the extent of the arbitrary decisions the leader can make and it means that all who are present have a part to play.

Worshippers can play an active part in different ways:

- One way is by allowing for, or relying on, spontaneous contributions, which support or determine the direction in which the act of worship moves. Quaker services are one example of this, and some churches deliberately allow time in worship for such things as the giving of testimony, the sharing of a 'prophecy' or some other message believed to be from God, or something as simple as suggesting the next song to sing.

- Another way is by planning in advance some particular parts for the congregation to play. Singing a hymn or song together is a simple example. Another example is the use of fixed forms of spoken words for the congregation, which could be either printed or known by heart. This sort of participation requires repeated actions and the use of existing words if it is truly to *belong* to the people corporately, rather than being determined by the leader or another individual.

Liturgy can encompass both forms of participation.

Liturgy is also corporate in the larger sense: it usually involves the wider Church, beyond the local congregation, in making at least some of the decisions. In this way the service does not belong to the local congregation alone, and especially not to the particular leader. There are agreed parts for the congregation which the leader is not at liberty to change or drop on a whim because they are known by everyone. There are parts of the service which are determined by the wider Church, usually via some sort of corporate decision-making body. Most of the differences between the denominations on questions of liturgy and worship are to do with who makes the decisions and how binding they are.

The content of corporate worship will inevitably be seen as an indication of what a particular congregation or denomination believes. This will be significant both to those who belong and to those who visit. In some denominations the liturgy is deliberately treated as one of the key places where you can see what the Church believes. This is why great care is taken over its production, and why there are limits placed on the amount of flexibility permitted at the local level.

Where are the decisions taken?

Roman Catholic
The decisions are made centrally and 'local' forms of service are translated from a normative Latin text and have to be approved by the Vatican. At parish level there is plenty of scope for choosing hymns and songs but few choices to be made about the form of service or the particular prayers used.

Church of England
Key decisions about structure and some texts are made centrally by the General Synod, working on material produced by the Liturgical Commission. At congregational level there is considerable freedom to choose between different forms of service and to decide which particular words are used. Decisions of principle (such as which form of communion service to use) are shared between the ordained leaders and the representatives of the laity (the Parochial Church

Council or its equivalent). Decisions about the detail (such as which form of confession to use) are taken by the person leading the service. For some elements there is limitless scope; for other elements (typically confessions, credal material and eucharistic prayers) the choice is more restricted.

Hymns and songs are unrestricted and a matter for local choice.

Methodist, United Reformed Church...

For some Free Churches there is a liturgy or a service book. It is usually drafted by a central committee or working group, often used experimentally, revised and then given official status by the governing body of the denomination. However, it is usually a matter for the local congregation to determine how closely to follow these services, what choices to make within them, and whether or not to use them at all.

Hymns and songs are a matter of local choice, but it is significant that these churches often produce 'official' hymn-books, over which considerable time and energy is expended.

Independent, 'New Church', Pentecostal...

These churches are likely to have no fixed forms of service and no printed resources. This means that local congregations are free to draw on the resources of other churches (or not) as they choose. Decisions are usually made by the leader of a particular service, and this means that the structure and patterns of worship tend to develop out of unspoken assumptions and ideas about what is right or appropriate. The network or denomination has little control over local worship except through informal networking and oversight.

Richly holistic

Sometimes those who have studied liturgy get bogged down in questions about the words that are used. Partly this is because of the importance that the Western Church since the Reformation has attached to words and the doctrines they reflect. The twentieth century, however, saw an important shift of attention among liturgical experts away from the words to the *shape* of worship. This was more than a concern for getting the order of things right.

It connected with fresh thinking about the physical aspects of worship: posture, movement, action, clothing, symbol, ritual, ceremonial, drama, and so on. People began to see that the space in which corporate worship takes place, the arrangement and nature of furniture within that space, and the mood set by music, lighting or smell, also has an impact on the worshippers and speaks volumes about God. Liturgy is an event in three dimensions, not a script on a page, and it should engage us as whole persons: body, mind and spirit.

Creative liturgy?

We have seen that liturgy should consciously connect our corporate gathering with that of other Christians in other places and other times, and should shape that gathering so that it forms us for living as Christian disciples.

Is it then possible to have 'creative liturgy'? Certainly it is possible to have new and 'creative' prayers to say, in the same way that you can have new songs to sing. But we have already seen that liturgy is much more than sets of spoken words. If liturgy is, by its very nature, handed on and connected to a tradition, then there is a sense in which 'creative liturgy' could be a contradiction in terms.

But we have also seen that there is little in the way of 'forms of service' given to us in Scripture. Throughout Church history, as well as around the world and in different churches today, Christians consider themselves to be worshipping 'in spirit and in truth' in many different ways.

Creative liturgy is possible – but it means more than writing new prayers and using more symbols and fresh imagery. To be creative with the liturgy requires an awareness of the riches of the Church's inheritance (across all traditions) and how that inheritance has developed, so that it can be drawn upon and used with integrity. It also requires a close contact with the contemporary context in which worship is to be offered. It needs a sense of drama and event, and of the deep structures of corporate worship. Above all, it needs to have an understanding of how meanings can be broken and remade by juxtaposing words and actions. This is liturgy's prophetic edge. Creative liturgy can never be truly Christian if it becomes an excuse for us to engage only with forms and words with which we feel comfortable: worship which is true to God, as well as true to us, must always stir us, call us and challenge us. To be re-shaped in the image of Christ is to be changed. That sort of liturgy is a dialogue with a living, developing tradition which seeks not to fossilize but to energize. Living, creative liturgy is the corporate worship of this congregation today, in dialogue with the Church universal in every time and place, which prepares us for the worship of eternity.

Conclusion

True liturgy

- empowers all God's people, not just leaders;

- connects with the past, and with the wider Church;

- engages the senses and uses symbolism and action as well as words;

- structures time and space to reflect the truths and priorities of God and his reign.

These are some of the primary aspects of liturgy.

Liturgical worship may, or may not, involve books, archaic language, special clothes, or elaborate ritual. All these things are secondary and not intrinsic to liturgy.

True liturgy will definitely be an event, a drama, in which all have a part to play, and which imprints on space and time the shape and pattern of the kingdom of God, which is here and yet to come.

For further reflection…

1. Reflect on your experiences of liturgical worship. What has been positive and what has been negative about them? Do you think your experiences reflect an encounter with the primary aspects of liturgy (structured, corporate, holistic), or with some of the secondary elements that sometimes become associated with liturgical worship?

2. Reflect on your experience of using books in worship (either for hymns and songs or for spoken words). How does using a book make you feel? Liberated? Frustrated? Constrained? Confused? Safe? Or something else? Why do you think that is?

3.   Reflect on ways in which the regular corporate worship
     which you have experienced has shaped your assumptions
     about God, Christianity and worship itself. If you have
     worshipped in different traditions, list them and compare
     them, noting anything that you felt was missing and anything
     that you felt was a gain in the different experiences.

3

Where does all this liturgy come from?

We have seen that liturgy is best thought of not as a collection of words to say or sing, nor as a particular form of service or style of doing things, but as worship with particular features:

■ clearly **structured**

■ essentially **corporate**

■ richly **holistic.**

We have also seen that because liturgical worship has a clear sense of connectedness with the wider Church beyond this time and place, it will inevitably be part of a developing tradition – it will have a history. In this chapter we ask where some of the key themes and features in liturgical worship come from and how we get the texts and actions that we inherit.

Case Study: How traditions in worship start and develop

Imagine a church. Advent is approaching and it is time for the construction of the Advent ring.

The person who normally makes the Advent ring has decided that the time has come to hand the job over to someone else, so the new person heads to the shops to buy some candles. She knows that, in her church, the four candles around the edge are normally purple and the one in the centre is white. She finds the white one without a problem, but can't find any shop that sells candles in the right sort of purple. Eventually she finds one shop that has purple candles, but they are the 'honeycomb' beeswax type. What should she do? She buys them and shows them to the vicar. 'They're not what we would normally use,' the vicar says, 'but they're quite appropriate in some ways – after all, in Advent we think about John the Baptist preparing the way for Jesus, and he ate wild honey. And we think about our waiting patiently for God's kingdom like the Israelites waiting to enter the land flowing with milk and honey. The beeswax can remind us of the honey bees. I think they'll be fine.' As it turns out, people rather like the link with John the Baptist.

And guess what? The next year they decide that it worked so well having the honeycomb candles that they do the same again.

Ten years later both the vicar and the person who first bought the honeycomb candles have moved on. No one else can remember where the idea of the honeycomb candles came from, but by now it has become a bit of a 'tradition' – it's just 'the way we do it here'. What is more, over the years, several people who have visited this church during Advent think that the honeycomb candles are a great idea. They take the idea back to their churches, so that twenty-five years later there are about thirty churches using honeycomb candles for Advent – and none of them knows why.

For better or worse, that's how liturgy, symbol and ceremonial can develop!

It is often extremely difficult to answer the simple question, 'Why do we do [or say] that?' Things that we do and say in church have sometimes been handed down for generations – or at least it seems that they have. Often they have been done for no more than a few decades, but no one can remember them starting and so people assume that they have 'always been done like that'.

On the whole, if you get several different answers when you ask the 'Why?' question, it's likely that the real or original answer has been lost. Very often words or actions in liturgy begin with a practical need – getting bread and wine to the table for communion, or lifting them up so that all can see them – but the practical need gets forgotten or is submerged by symbolic meanings added afterwards. Sometimes the practical purpose is no longer relevant, but the symbol persists. Candles were first used in churches primarily to give light. Later they came to be seen as symbols of the light of Christ. Though electric light has taken over the practical purpose, candles still retain the symbolic meaning.

Saying that something was originally practical and has now become symbolic (often with competing meanings) does not necessarily mean that we shouldn't do it any more or that it is not helpful. It does mean that we need to be cautious about declaring the absolute meanings of things and willing to see that new meanings can be added and that new symbols, actions and words may replace them. The phrase, 'We've always done it this way' is never true – you simply need to go back a bit further to discover how it was done before it was done 'this way'.

Case Study: Wine and water

When I first started going to church, I noticed that the wine for Holy Communion was mixed with a little water. When I asked why, I got the following answers from different people:

- *To symbolize the blood and water which came out when the spear was pushed into the side of Jesus on the cross;*

- *To symbolize the two 'natures' of Christ: that he was both human and divine;*

- *To save money on wine(!).*

Originally wine and water were probably mixed at communion simply because at the time of Christ and the early Church wine was always mixed with water when it was drunk at ordinary meals. Wine was stored as a thick liquid that needed to be diluted in order to be drunk. Early accounts of the Eucharist sometimes mention the water used with the wine, but don't give any particular meaning to it, probably because the writers simply take it for granted as a normal practice without symbolic significance. Nowadays, of course, we don't usually water down wine when we drink it socially, and you can understand why someone seeing it happen might think that the Church is just saving money. But that doesn't necessarily mean that it is a bad symbol. If people can see in it something true, then it may be a help to them in thinking about Christ at communion. It may, however, become a bad symbol if a false or misleading message is picked up.

Beginnings

We have already seen that the New Testament does not give us a simple order of service, or some words that we can include in our services, or some basic ceremonial. Nonetheless, the natural expectation might be that if you went far enough back you would find that the diversity of worship in the Church today could all be traced back to some basic forms from which they developed.

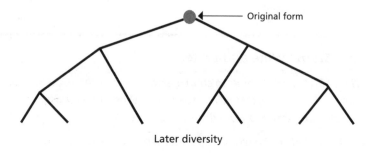

Figure 1: From simplicity to diversity

For a long time that's exactly what liturgical scholars and historians thought. All their assumptions were based on the idea that original simplicity developed over time into greater complexity. This affected how they interpreted the bits of historical evidence they found. If it looked fairly simple the assumption was that this was an early text; more complicated forms were assumed to be later, and so on.

Knowing what we don't know

In more recent years scholars have realized that we know less than we thought we did about Christian worship in the early centuries of the Christian era (and about the Jewish worship from which, it is assumed, much of it developed). Much of the evidence that we do have has been reassessed and we have learnt to be more careful about some of the assumptions we make.

What has emerged is a much more complicated picture. For a start, there seems to have been no simple 'source' from which other forms of worship developed. Certainly there are common elements. Most of the first Christians were Jews and their faith was formed in a Jewish context. Jesus himself was a Jew and, though he had much to criticize in the way the leaders of his day controlled the Jewish religion, he stressed again and again that he had not come to abolish it but to fulfil it. He himself took part in worship in temple and synagogue.

Three centres of worship

Jews had three places where their worship was focused:

- the temple
- the synagogue
- the home

The temple was a centre of sacrifice with an aristocratic hereditary priesthood in charge. It was also a focus for prayer and Jews gathered in the outer courts to pray at the same time as the sacrifices were taking place inside (see, for instance, Luke 1.10 and Acts 3.1). The Romans destroyed the Jerusalem temple in AD 70, and from that time the other two centres of worship took on a more significant role.

We have little definite information about worship in the synagogues at the time of Jesus. What we do know is that these were centres of worship which did not require the presence or leadership of priests. Worship in the synagogue consisted of readings from the Hebrew Scriptures (what Christians came to call the 'Old Testament') and prayers.

Of the three, perhaps the key centre for Jewish worship was the home. It was here that prayers were said, religious ceremonies took place (such as the Passover) and the faith was passed on to the next generation in story, symbol and ritual.

Christian developments

There is not room here for a thorough history of the development of Christian worship (see the Appendix for ideas for further reading). Instead, we're going to take a very quick overview, focusing on some of the significant points at which there was a change of direction or emphasis.

In the early days of the Church the followers of Jesus, like other Jews, gathered at the temple for prayer (Acts 3.1 and 5.12). Later, it seems that Christians may have set up 'rival' synagogues on a similar model to the Jewish ones. But crucial to understanding early Christian worship is seeing the importance of the home. Jesus gathered round him an extended family of disciples. Many of them had travelled with him in his ministry. They had eaten together and he had spoken of them as his family (Mark 3.34, 35). After his resurrection many of the encounters with the risen Jesus took place in domestic settings and in the context of meals. After Jesus' ascension the believers continued to meet together, with the home as a key centre (e.g. Acts 2.46). It was here that the stories of Jesus were probably first passed on. It was here that prayers were first said 'in the name of Jesus', perhaps in the early days adapting prayers that were already familiar to Jews. And here the believers first began to remember Jesus in blessing God for food and sharing bread and wine at meal times. This is probably the reason why there is so little in the New Testament about meetings for 'worship' as we would think of it; it was taken for granted and took place primarily in the small and informal settings of household prayers, shared meals and so on.

What did the early Christians do?

We have no firm evidence of what went on in the homes of the early Christians when they met – just the most tantalizing of glimpses, mentioned in passing in the Acts of the Apostles and the letters of the New Testament (see above, pages 3–4). No basic form of worship is spelt out for us and there is no evidence of any uniformity in how these elements were combined in the different places where God was worshipped through Christ. And it doesn't get much clearer if we look further into the first two centuries after Christ.

Worship in the empire

As the Christian faith spread around the Roman empire the Church had to engage with cultures that had other ideas about what worship entailed. We see hints of this in Paul's first letter to the Christians at Corinth. This particularly addresses things that were going wrong in Corinth, such as inappropriate behaviour at the Lord's Supper (see 1 Corinthians 11). The destruction of Jerusalem by the Romans in AD 70 (including the temple there) added to the non-Jewish influence on the Christian Church by increasing the speed at which Christians were dispersed around the empire, as they, along with other Jews, were sent out from Jerusalem.

The caricature of Christians worshipping in dark catacombs for fear of the authorities is only partly right. The persecution of Christians was worse in some places than others and at some times than others.

Some Christians were worshipping in secret for much of the time, but the most common place for worship in the empire was not the catacomb or the secret open-air rendezvous, but the home. Christians commonly met in the apartment blocks of the large cities and the spacious dwellings of the provincial towns.

And still we don't know exactly what went on. Justin Martyr, a second-century writer who explained and defended the Christian faith to non-Christians, includes an account of Christian worship in a couple of places in his writings. Tantalizingly, he gives us outlines, not details. He mentions readings but does not say who reads them. He mentions what we would call a sermon, but says only that it lasts 'as long as there is time for' (perhaps we could do with more of that today!). And of the prayer over the bread and wine he states that the leader (who he calls the 'president') prays 'to the best of his ability'.

We don't know to what degree his account is typical of Christian worship all over the empire, but it at least gives a glimpse of what was happening in one place.

We get a similar picture in a piece of writing from about AD 215, called *The Apostolic Tradition*, often ascribed to Hippolytus, a bishop in Rome in the third century. The writer describes what happens (or what he thought *ought* to happen – we don't really know) at the consecration of a bishop. Again, when it comes to the prayer over the bread and wine in the Holy Communion (the part of the service over which modern Christians often argue the most, trying to get the words right) the writer simply gives a form of words that could be used by leaders who were not able to come up with something better themselves. It seems that the idea was: 'If you have the ability, then make up your own prayer: if not, then use a prayer from someone who does have the ability.'

All change?

This attitude was set to change. One of the key factors in that change was that the emperor, Constantine, became a Christian himself, having ascribed his victory at the Battle of Milvian Bridge in AD 312 to the God of the Christians.

Not only did he become a Christian, but he took a rather keen interest in things to do with the Church. It did not happen overnight, but over time the situation for the Church changed considerably.

No longer a sporadically persecuted minority, Christians were first tolerated and then favoured. Christianity was made the state religion in AD 380. What is more, with the state taking an active interest in what went on in worship, it became very important to get it 'right'. The development of formal statements of 'orthodox' doctrine influenced worship, making fixed and uniform liturgies seem a sensible precaution.

This brought considerable change to Christian worship. What had basically been a domestic event became a large-scale public event, in which church leaders were taking on the role of important civic leaders as well. Christians began to build church buildings for worship and modelled them, not on the pagan temples, but on the basilica, the empire's spaces for secular government and meetings. This was the equivalent of us modelling our churches on a cross between the town hall and the out-of-town shopping centre.

Some other things that are often associated with Christian worship developed at this time:

- **Vestments and robes:** Christian leaders began to wear special clothes, like the magistrates and other important civic leaders. Outdoor clothes began to be worn indoors for processions in the large church buildings. Most of the ecclesiastical clothes commonly worn by clergy today (cassocks, surplices, chasubles, stoles, etc.) have their origins in the formal Roman dress of the fourth and fifth centuries. With the conservatism inherent in public ceremonial, when everyone else stopped wearing these clothes, Christian leaders continued to wear them in worship. The formal robes worn today by, for instance, judges have a similar origin.

- **Processions with candles and crosses:** Roman civic leaders processed through the streets with the symbols of their office, lights and incense. Christian leaders began to do likewise and take the procession into the church buildings, where, naturally enough, Christian symbolism began to be attached to the various actions and objects.

Another significant change was the growth of Christian travel, the pilgrimage. Just like the groups today that go away to Lourdes, Taizé, Spring Harvest or Iona, and then want to reproduce their experience back home, Christians in the fourth and fifth centuries began to travel and bring back to their homes the great ideas they saw in worship in other places. In particular they began to bring back ideas from the great centres of Christianity such as Jerusalem, Alexandria and Rome. Here we see the reverse of our original assumption that simplicity developed into diversity. At this stage diverse practices in worship tended to converge as people copied what was happening at these great centres. This is how the 'families' of forms of worship developed: forms that were like the worship at Rome; forms that were like the services at Alexandria; and so on.

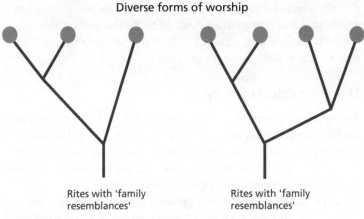

Figure 2: From diversity to 'families'

The Middle Ages

By the peak of the Middle Ages Christian worship in the West had become pretty complicated. Lots of extras had been added to the basic elements of Christian worship. Some of these were good and helpful; others seemed to crowd out the key elements, some of which almost became lost. The medieval Mass gained introits (chants which were sung as the ministers entered the church in procession), confessions, and secret prayers said by the priest. It lost the sermon; the peace was just a remnant, shared only between the clergy; and the people no longer received the bread and wine in communion. The Mass dominated worship and, for the laity, the word-based services of prayer and praise were lost.

Of course, there was also plenty that was good: renewal movements such as the Franciscans revived preaching and great hymns were being written, but much of this was outside the main liturgy, or supplemented it.

The Reformation arrived like a bulldozer clearing a beach. The intention of the Reformers was to clear away what they saw as debris and reveal the 'simplicity' of early Christian worship which they believed lay beneath it. They renamed the Mass, calling it the Lord's Supper or Holy Communion, a change of name which reflected a shift of emphasis. Eating bread and drinking wine together in remembrance of Jesus was recovered as the key element of the service. Services of word and prayer also got a higher profile, not least because of the Reformers' emphasis on preaching. Changed doctrine was reflected and reinforced by the new forms of service, which gave a very prominent position to the doctrines closest to the Reformers' hearts, such as the centrality of the cross and the importance of faith alone for salvation.

The ecumenical century

If we shift our attention from the sixteenth to the twentieth century, we find a drawing together of some of the traditions that were divided so strongly at the Reformation. The end of the nineteenth century and the start of the twentieth century marked the beginning of what came to be known as the Liturgical Movement. It began among French Roman Catholic Benedictines who were seeking to discover and recover the roots of their own monastic worship tradition. In the process they discovered much about the Church's wider liturgical heritage, and the movement they sparked grew to influence liturgical thinking all over Europe and the Western world.

The Liturgical Movement was concerned both with the connection between liturgy and Christian discipleship, and with the need for solid theological and historical foundations in the understanding of worship. It began with a focus on liturgy in the Middle Ages, which connected with the general revival of interest at the time in the art and architecture of the medieval period. But fresh historical discoveries were being made (including early church documents and architectural remains) and more refined and technical approaches to the study of ancient texts were being applied to liturgical texts. This led to a shift of focus in the Liturgical Movement, which turned its attention to the patterns of worship in the early centuries of the Church. This was more conducive to the increasingly ecumenical climate, because it reached back to the time before the divisions of the Reformation period and before the separation of East and West. It seemed to offer models of worship around which large numbers of Christians could unite. The fact that this Liturgical Movement grew hand in hand with the Ecumenical Movement proved to be its greatest strength. Each influenced the other.

Because so much of the new thinking about worship was done ecumenically, many modern forms of service, and some of the words within those forms, are shared across the denominations.

Key features of the twentieth-century Liturgical Movement

- A deeper sense of community and of public worship as an activity of the whole people of God;

- a stress on active participation by the people, reflected in a greater concern for the part played by the congregation and wider leadership roles for lay people alongside ordained ministers;

- the use of vernacular languages and an engagement with local culture in acts of worship;

- a clearer sense that what happens in worship should connect with the Church's life in the world;

- a recovery in all denominations of the importance of the Eucharist ('the Lord's Supper') as the appropriate main service on 'the Lord's Day'.

- a parallel recovery of the importance of the Bible within worship and in forming worship.

Much liturgical revision in the twentieth century was the result of this new thinking – and new discoveries about the shape of early Christian worship – finding their way into new forms of service.

As we take a bird's-eye view of the history of Christian worship, what we see is not a clear development in a constant line from Jesus to today, but a complex network of influences producing different patterns of worship in different places and at different times.

Scholars sometimes refer to these as 'families' of rites. Each of these has a fairly stable structure, which is done in a particular way and with recognizable words. Sometimes these families have been determined by geography; sometimes they have been determined by doctrinal or ecclesiological divisions (such as the division between Eastern and Western Christianity or the Catholic/Protestant divide within Western Christianity). Today the most obvious divide in liturgical families is between those who consider that their worship is liturgical (and among these there has been great convergence) and those who aim to be 'free' of liturgical 'constraints'. Even this divide has been breached in recent years as liturgical and non-liturgical traditions have begun to encounter and value one another's insights and strengths in an increasingly ecumenical (some would say 'post-denominational') context.

The living tradition of liturgy has often developed rather like waves washing in on the shore: the shore is stable in the short term, but over the long term you can see that each new wave brings in new material and takes away other material. Rubbish sometimes gets deposited after a storm; at other times large amounts of the cliff may crumble into the sea. Sand from further round the coast may get deposited on the beach. Over long periods of time considerable changes take place but it is only clearly discernible with the benefit of hindsight. And different beaches change at different paces. In the Eastern churches change has been very slow and forms of service used today have a very clear connection with those that have been used for hundreds of years. Indeed, these archaic forms are deliberately preserved in order to portray 'another world' – the heavenly world with which we connect in worship. In the Western churches we have become used to worship changing (though not always very often) due either to doctrinal tumult, as during the Reformation, or to cultural shifts and changes such as the modern shift towards more informality in public life.

Sharing the work

There are significant ecumenical organizations which have fostered the work of liturgical renewal.

- **The Joint Liturgical Group (JLG):** this British group, with representatives from the main denominations, was set up in the 1960s and has produced orders of service, lectionaries and key thinking which has influenced the liturgical revision of individual churches.

- **The Churches' Consultation on Texts (CCT):** this North American forum produced the ecumenical *Common Lectionary* in the 1980s.

- **The English Language Liturgical Consultation (ELLC):** this international organization (with representatives from national bodies such as JLG and CCT) has produced English translations of key texts (such as the creeds and the Lord's Prayer) for the use of the churches of the English-speaking world. It was also responsible for producing the ecumenical three-year *Revised Common Lectionary* in 1992, which has been adopted by many Churches of different traditions around the world.

There is a temptation to talk about *the* liturgy rather than liturgy – as if liturgy was one fixed thing, the 'right' way of doing things. This has contributed, among some Christians, to the image of liturgy as being about services which are archaic, dull, repetitive, irrelevant and predetermined to the point of squeezing out any spontaneity. Such a view can de-skill worshippers by giving the impression that worship belongs to those 'who know' rather than those who pray. This is to turn true liturgy upside down.

The fact that liturgy connects us with other times and places need not result in the one-dimensional view that there is one 'right' or best liturgy, to which all other worship should tend if it is to be pleasing to God. Historic research has shown the folly of searching for the original 'pure' liturgy. The modern ecumenical context means that Christians in all churches are now more familiar with the way other Christians worship, and are therefore able to comment on other patterns (and perhaps to consider and constructively criticize their own worshipping tradition) from a position of knowledge rather than ignorance or fear.

Such openness to considering both the strengths and weaknesses of our own preferences and inherited patterns should result in worship which is, more than ever, in 'spirit and in truth' – having integrity with both the real situation of the worshippers and the true nature of the God whom we worship.

For further reflection...

1. What do you consider to be the greatest strengths of the worship in your own church? What are the weaknesses? Have you experienced worship in another church or tradition? If so, how has that affected your assessment of the worship in your present church?

2. Are there actions, words or symbols in the worship of your church that you don't understand? Who could you ask, or where could you go to find out more about them?

3. Are there actions or symbols used in your church that you think might be conveying positively harmful messages to those who don't understand what they are meant to represent? Can you think of alternative actions or symbols (or changes to the current ones) that would convey the intended meaning(s) more effectively?

4. Can you think of any entirely practical actions that are part of the services at your church, which, in a hundred years' time when no one can remember their origin, might be given symbolic meaning?

4

Where does the Eucharist come from?

Two sorts of worship

The first Christians seem to have had two main focuses
for their public worship:

- the fellowship meal (which later developed into what
  we would think of as Holy Communion);

- gatherings focused on prayer and the reading of Scripture.

This second focus seems to have drawn on the worship pattern of
the synagogue and the daily domestic prayer of every Jewish family.
In content it included singing, the reading and exposition of Scripture
and the use of familiar prayers. We may perhaps see echoes of this
sort of gathering in the reference in Ephesians 5.18-20 ('psalms,
hymns and spiritual songs') and in 1 Corinthians 14.26:

> When you come together, each one has a hymn, a lesson,
> a revelation, a tongue, or an interpretation. Let all things
> be done for building up.

However, it is the former sort of worship, the fellowship meal
that developed into what we now call the Eucharist (or Holy
Communion, or the Mass, or the Lord's Supper – see below) that
has come to dominate both the worship of the majority of Christian
churches and the study of liturgy and worship. In the previous
chapter we considered how liturgy in general develops, and how
Christian worship has been shaped over the last two thousand
years. In this chapter we give special attention to how the Eucharist
has developed.

What did Jesus think he was starting?

Although Jesus, at the Last Supper, told his disciples to 'do this in remembrance of me', we have little clear idea of

- exactly what he expected them to do (other than that it would involve bread and wine); or

- how often he expected them to do it (Paul, and Paul alone, records simply that Jesus said, 'as often as you drink it' – 1 Corinthians 11.25); or

- in what context it was to be done (the Last Supper itself was not a public act of worship, though it took place in the context of a religious 'rite').

Even its name has been a source of controversy – and the amount of controversy that has always surrounded the Eucharist is a sign of just how important it has been to Christians. Jesus' command to 'do this in remembrance of me' has been followed, but in diverse ways and with considerable differences of understanding at different times and in different places. In this chapter we use the Eucharist as a 'case study' in just how particular forms of liturgy can develop and change over time.

What's in a name?

There are many different names used for the service. The terms used by different churches often give clues to the particular emphases which they put on the service.

- **Lord's Supper:** used in the New Testament (for instance, 1 Corinthians 11.20) and reflects the origin of the service in a meal.

- **The Breaking of Bread:** a New Testament term which could mean simply 'sharing a meal' but seems to be used as a technical term for the special meal at which Jesus is remembered (see Luke 24.30, 35; Acts 2.42 and 20.7). It puts the emphasis on the action and is a term often used by churches with a strong evangelical tradition.

- **Eucharist:** from the Greek word for 'thanksgiving'. Originally a reference to giving thanks to God over the bread and wine and later extended to become a way of referring to the whole service. It has become the most commonly used term in ecumenical circles, as it is not closely associated with any one Church or tradition.

■ **Holy Communion:** that is, 'holy fellowship', emphasizing the special sense of belonging together with the risen Lord and with one another.

■ **The Mass:** the origins of this term are not clear, but the most likely answer is that it is a corruption of the final 'dismissal' in the Latin service: 'Ite, missa est' – 'Go, it is over'.

■ **The Holy Mysteries:** a term more common in the Eastern churches; it fits in with their emphasis on the mystery of the Eucharist, in which we are caught up into the worship of heaven.

The roots of the Eucharist

We do not even know exactly what sort of meal the Last Supper was. It is often assumed that it was a Passover meal, and that is how Matthew, Mark and Luke portray it in their Gospels. John, on the other hand, does not record the Last Supper in detail at all – his emphasis is on the washing of the disciples' feet and he has the meal taking place *before* the Passover (John 13.1). In his account, Jesus, the Lamb of God (John 1.36), is being crucified on the day on which the Passover lambs are being slaughtered. Though the Gospel accounts have the disciples going to prepare the Passover, in none of the accounts of the Last Supper is the detail of the Passover meal itself given – they all simply refer to 'the supper' in order to give some context to the actions with the bread and wine.

Bread and wine are elements of a normal Jewish meal, and not particular to the Passover at all. In fact, the 'Lord's Supper' in the early Church seems to have developed out of a whole range of associations between Jesus and eating and drinking:

■ **Jesus' meals with 'saints and sinners':** eating with people was a regular part of Jesus' life and ministry, and a key sign of his acceptance of those often treated as outcasts. For instance, the banquet given by Levi the tax collector (Luke 5.27-38); at the home of Simon the Pharisee (Luke 7.36-50); with Mary, Martha and Lazarus (John 12.1-3); at the home of Simon who had leprosy (Matthew 26.6-13); having tea with Zacchaeus (Luke 19.1-10).

- **Jesus' teaching about the heavenly banquet:** the picture of the kingdom of God as a feast or wedding banquet is part of Jesus' teaching (see, for instance: Matthew 8.11;, 22.1-13 and 25.1-13; Luke 14.15-24).

- **The miraculous feedings:** the feeding of the 5,000 is the only miracle story of Jesus which is recorded in all four Gospels, and was itself a reflection and a sign of the overflowing abundance of the kingdom of God, the heavenly banquet.

  In John's account, it is followed by significant teaching from Jesus about 'eating his flesh and drinking his blood' (John 6.53-56) which takes place at a time when the Passover festival was near. There are strong echoes here of Jesus' words at the Last Supper, as recorded by Matthew, Mark and Luke, when he associates bread with his body and wine with his blood.

- **The resurrection meals:** several of Jesus' resurrection appearances are accompanied by eating:

  - the breakfast of fish and bread by the lake (John 21.1-14);

  - the meal with the two disciples at Emmaus, during which Jesus is revealed to them 'in the breaking of the bread' (Luke 24.28-35);

  - the appearance in the upper room when Jesus eats in front of them (Luke 24.36-43).

- **The Last Supper and the Passover:** whether the Last Supper was an actual Passover meal or not, it clearly took place in the context of the Passover season, in which the Jews were used to the idea of food being used in powerfully symbolic ways. And yet, Jesus chose not to give new meaning to the lamb of the Passover, or the bitter herbs, but to use the more ordinary elements of bread and wine, which were part of normal meals.

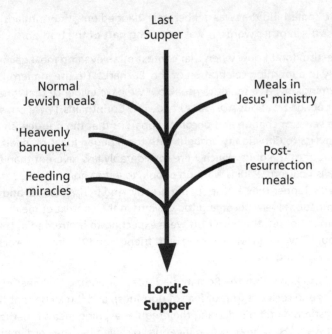

Figure 3: Roots of the Eucharist

When the first Christians began to keep the Lord's Supper as a regular 'ritual' they did so, at first, in the context of a normal meal. This means that it might have taken place several times a week, perhaps at every meal, in the very domestic setting of the first Christians gathering in their homes to remember Jesus (Acts 2.46). It was as if they were conscious of the risen Lord with them then, just as he had been in Galilee, and just as he had been in those resurrection appearances: their meals in remembrance of Jesus were a declaration of continuity – he is still here!

When a more formal pattern of sharing the Lord's Supper developed, it is significant that it was a weekly pattern (on the Lord's Day) rather than an annual celebration like the Passover.

We don't know for sure when the informal sharing of a meal, at which Jesus was remembered in bread and wine, developed into a more formal ritual (still, at first, in the context of a meal). We know that by the time Paul was writing to the church at Corinth (probably about AD 50) the Lord's Supper was already becoming formalized into something that was deliberately 'handed on' (1 Corinthians 11.23) – in other words, it was becoming part of the tradition.

We also don't know when that context of an evening meal gave way to a morning celebration of the 'Eucharist' (to use modern terminology) as a separate ritual, but we have evidence that it had happened by about AD 150. Already in 1 Corinthians 11 we can see the seeds of change as it becomes apparent that the non-Jewish converts to Christianity brought with them pagan ideas of meals in honour of the gods, which were considerably less reverent than the Jewish pattern. Paul is warning people to eat at home, so that at the Lord's Supper they are not being greedy. And perhaps social and class distinctions were becoming too obvious in the context of meals in Roman houses: the better off were expecting to be treated as they would have been when dining with friends, and the lower classes were getting the left-overs.

We also know that the Romans had rules forbidding the meeting of clubs and societies (out of fear of uprisings), and it may be that the Christians didn't mind losing their regular evening meals together, but were less willing to stop meeting to remember the Lord in bread and wine.

Whatever the reasons, by the middle of the second century it looks as though a meal was no longer the normal or regular context in which the Eucharist was celebrated.

Justin Martyr's account

Justin was a Christian writer who tried to explain the Christian religion to those outside the Church, both Jew and Gentile. From his writings, in about AD 150, we can piece together some aspects of the Eucharist as Justin experienced it and as he described it to others. We can't be sure how typical his account is, or how much he put a 'spin' on it in order to portray Christianity in a good light, but these are the elements he mentions:

- the Christians gather in the morning;

- the leader of the act of worship is called the 'president';

- there are readings from what we would call the 'New Testament' ('the writings of the apostles') and possibly the Old Testament (he refers to the writings of the 'prophets', though we don't know if this means the Hebrew prophets or prophets in the early Church);

- a sermon is given by the president;

- the people pray together;

- the 'peace' is shared ('we salute one another with a kiss');

- bread and wine are brought to the table;

- the president gives thanks over the bread and wine;

- the bread and wine are distributed to those present and deacons take it to those who are not present (perhaps prevented by sickness or imprisonment);

- there is a collection!

If this all sounds very familiar, it simply shows that small pieces of evidence like this have been extremely influential in the renewal of the Eucharist over the last century.

As the centuries rolled on towards the medieval period, the Eucharist gained and lost various elements as it became more and more central to Christian worship. Not only did certain key things almost disappear (the sermon, for instance), but other items were added (such as extra prayers, sentences of Scripture and anthems) and the basic shape of the service got submerged so that it was barely recognizable.

More significantly, the Eucharist in the West became increasingly focused on remembering the Last Supper and the death of Jesus, and bringing that unique eternal sacrifice into the present through the consecration of the bread and wine. The forward-looking emphasis of the New Testament and the early Church (that the supper was a foretaste of the heavenly banquet) had been overtaken by a focus on bringing the past into the present, rather than pointing the present to the future. Paul's teaching holds the two together:

> For as often as you eat this bread and drink the cup,
> you proclaim the Lord's death *until he comes*.

> *1 Corinthians 11.26 [emphasis added]*

The 'sacrifice of the Mass' proclaimed (or even, in some understandings, offered) the Lord's death, but there was little focus on his coming again.

By the Middle Ages the experience for the members of the congregation focused on the miracle of Christ becoming present on the altar when the words of consecration were spoken. Because the services were still in Latin, even when most ordinary people no longer spoke it, bells were rung at the key moments so that the people knew when to look up and recognize the presence of Christ. The focus on the physical elements themselves (rather than the action of eating and drinking) led to the bread and wine being treated with greater and greater reverence. From the fourth century onwards there is evidence that the fear of receiving communion 'unworthily' (1 Corinthians 11.27) was leading some people to refuse the bread and wine of communion. In the medieval period this fear had become widespread. By the end of the thirteenth century the laity were ordinarily denied the wine of communion altogether, for fear of spillages. Even the bread was received only rarely by laypeople – perhaps twice a year, at Christmas and Easter.

When the Reformation hit the Church in Europe in the sixteenth century, the agenda went far beyond the liturgy, but the Reformers saw the renewal of worship as a key part of the renewal of the Church. They wanted both to restore the sense of the Eucharist as a meal in which all participate (hence their preference for titles like 'Lord's Supper' and 'Holy Communion', rather than 'Mass') and also to use it to reinforce the doctrines of justification by faith and the importance of the Bible. The key changes to the services were:

■ simplification;

■ use of vernacular languages, such as English, rather than Latin;

■ greater active participation by the congregation;

■ reception of both bread and wine by the congregation every time.

The Reformers were not against sacraments. They were convinced that the Lord's Supper should be celebrated regularly, normally every Sunday. They wanted the people to share in the bread and wine, but they found the people unwilling, after centuries of restrictions. And so a regular pattern of non-eucharistic worship developed as the norm on Sundays, with Holy Communion being seen as a rare occurrence for which considerable preparation was necessary.

It is only in the last fifty years that the original vision of the Reformers has been fulfilled, as churches which stand in the Reformation traditions have rediscovered the Eucharist and affirmed again its importance as a regular, even weekly, service. This has come about largely through the more positive ecumenical atmosphere: churches have become more able to listen and learn from one another and to affirm the positive in each other's practices.

Ecumenical convergence

The twentieth century saw a growth in ecumenical working in many areas of church life, and worship was no exception. The most significant impact of the Liturgical Movement, which we encountered in Chapter 3, was on the renewal of the Eucharist. New discoveries (of early church documents) and a new emphasis on the action of the Eucharist, rather than simply the words, led to a lot of common thinking about the structure of the Eucharist and some agreement over forms of words for key parts of the service. Ecumenical theological work about the meaning of the Eucharist (by, for instance, the Anglican–Roman Catholic International Commission (ARCIC) and the World Council of Churches) also helped; it enabled different denominations to affirm the points on which they agreed and share points on which they were happy to differ, as well as clarifying the areas on which there is still considerable disagreement.

In 1948 the Church of South India was formed by bringing together Anglicans, Methodists, Congregationalists and Presbyterians. In 1952 it produced new forms of service and became the first Church to put the new thinking about the Eucharist into liturgical form, especially the new (or 'classic') shape for the service (see Chapter 8, pp. 90–91).

In the 1960s the Roman Catholic Church's Second Vatican Council began to apply the new principles of the Liturgical Movement in its *Constitution on the Sacred Liturgy*, the first document to emerge from the Council's work. This in turn influenced the thinking of those in other churches who tended to look to Rome for guidance on matters liturgical.

At the grass-roots level, Christians sharing in worship (whether in joint services, or in the growing number of 'ecumenical partnership' churches) discovered a unity in their worship which acted as a catalyst to the wider ecumenical work on theology.

For further reflection...

1. If somebody asked you what the Eucharist is for, what would you say in response? If they then pressed you to explain how it does this, would you have an answer?

2. Are there things about the way the Eucharist is celebrated in your own church and tradition about which you now realize you would like to find out more?

5

Liturgy and the ordering of time

We have seen that liturgy is not a fixed way of doing things, but an approach to corporate worship. In Chapter 2 we saw that it is about bringing (or reflecting) the order of God's kingdom in powerful, living and symbolic ways, in our lives and in the space and time in which we worship God together. Well, that's the theory at least! In this chapter we look at the most basic structuring of all: the ordering of time itself in the day, the week and the annual calendar.

Finding our place in time

Life sometimes feels like a curious combination of going round in circles and yet moving inexorably forward to our final destination. This applies to individuals, to particular communities and to human society itself.

Often the sense of recurring patterns and the sense of a clear destination are connected. We are conscious of key stages in our lives, such as birth, coming of age, changing jobs (or finding work), setting up home, forming relationships with others, giving birth, moving home, leaving a job, retirement, and so on. Many of these occasions are marked by the giving of gifts or cards, by parties or other celebrations. Equally, we celebrate annually the *anniversary* of many of those stages and these give a sense of rhythm to the year and our lives: our birthday comes around again; we celebrate a wedding anniversary; perhaps we recall the birthday of a deceased parent, partner or child. Whether happy or sad, these signposts combine the cyclic and linear aspects of our lives. Each year they come round. They give us a sense of where we are in the year and where we are in our lives: How many years since that event? How have we changed in the intervening period? And so on.

In worship it is possible to see three levels at which this sense of rhythm and forward movement takes place:

- the day

- the week

- the year.

The day: light and dark

From the creation of the world, each day brings a rhythm of darkness and night: 'There was evening and there was morning, the first day' (Genesis 1.5).

It seems that the first Christians wanted to 'pray without ceasing' (1 Thessalonians 5.17) and one way of doing this was to follow the Jewish pattern of using the natural rhythm of the day as a trigger for prayer. At first it seems that the followers of the risen Christ prayed at least twice a day, morning and evening, at the times of the sacrifices in the Jerusalem temple. They also followed the Jewish practice of praying at meal times. They prayed together, at first in homes and at the temple and, after the conversion of Emperor Constantine in the fourth century, publicly in church buildings.

In different contexts and at different times in history, the pattern has been elaborated (for instance, the eightfold monastic pattern) or simplified (for instance, the twofold pattern of Morning and Evening Prayer in the Church of England's *Book of Common Prayer*).

Even today, when electric light has removed some of the obvious symbolism of sunrise in the morning and the lighting of lamps at evening, there are three times of day with an obvious focus for prayer:

- first thing in the morning, as we look ahead to what the day holds;

- in the middle of the day, in the midst of work and activity;

- at the end of the day, before sleep, as a way of committing to God all that has taken place.

Two basic patterns

Although there has been enormous diversity in the Church about patterns of daily prayer, scholars have identified two basic historical patterns, with distinct emphases, which continue to influence current thinking and assumptions.

- **An 'urban' pattern:** this was the earliest pattern, which developed in the towns and cities and after the fourth century was focused on the cathedral or major church. It was essentially corporate and 'outward-looking', focusing on corporate praise and intercession.

- **A 'monastic' pattern:** this originated in the prayer of those who chose the life of a hermit or a 'religious' community. It was primarily 'inward-looking', focused on the individual's spiritual development, largely through reading and meditating on Scripture. In later centuries the individual emphasis came to dominate the understanding of regular daily prayer, even in the towns and cities.

The use of the psalms

The psalms have traditionally been seen as a key part of the daily prayer of Christians. But the way that the psalms were used was different in the two patterns.

- In the 'urban' pattern the psalms were seen primarily as part of the praise and thanksgiving; the book of Psalms acted as a sort of 'hymn-book' from which appropriate psalms were chosen to suit the time of day or the season of the year. Other psalms or parts of psalms might not be used at all.

- In the 'monastic' pattern the psalms were seen as a resource for meditation, part of the story of God's people, reflecting different emotions and *all* used in a regular pattern.

The two different approaches are reflected in the different ways the psalms have been and are used:

- The 'urban' pattern has seen something of a revival in some recent forms of daily prayer (such as *Celebrating Common Prayer*, and the seasonal parts of the Church of England's *Common Worship* weekday lectionary). In these, the psalms are chosen for their appropriateness to the time of day or the season of the year. In Advent, for instance, a limited selection of psalms is chosen which connect with the traditional themes of the Advent season – watching and waiting in joyful hope.

- In the Church of England's *Book of Common Prayer*, by contrast, the psalms are distributed in their biblical order over Morning and Evening Prayer for a month so that a regular worshipper will be exposed to all 150 (with their many different themes and moods) in the space of 30 days. The *Common Worship* weekday lectionary takes a similar approach outside the great seasons of the Church's year. This is much closer to the 'monastic' pattern.

The tension between the two approaches can also be seen in the different views among Christians about whether the psalms should be used in their entirety or whether some psalms (the so-called 'cursing psalms'), or parts of psalms, should be omitted. At root it is a debate about whether the psalms give us words which we can make our own in our praise and prayer without qualification, or whether they are part of an engagement with the whole of Scripture, 'warts and all', primarily for reflection. The use of a 'psalm prayer' or the 'Glory to the Father' at the end of the psalm (which puts the psalm in a Christian context) is also a reflection of that complex relationship between the psalms and the Christian faith: whatever the sentiments expressed in the psalm, they are not, for Christians, the last word. It is Christ and what he reveals about God that completes the picture.

The week: work and rest

The pattern of 'the week', like the pattern of the day, also finds its origins in the book of Genesis, in God's own pattern of six days of work followed by a day of rest. It was a pattern intended to be followed by humankind, who are made in the image of God; the seventh day was a day both to rest from labour and to 'give to the Lord'.

The early Christians, being Jews, were familiar with this idea, but for them the key day in the week became not Saturday (the Jewish Sabbath) but Sunday, the first day of the week, the day of resurrection. Sunday became known among Christians as 'the Lord's day' (Revelation 1.10) and when Christians began to meet formally it was on the Lord's day that they did so (Acts 20.7). It wasn't a public holiday at first, but a normal working day, so Christians had to gather either very early in the day before work began, or in the evening. It was also popular among Christian teachers to refer to Sunday as 'the eighth day'. For Jewish Christians this made the contrast clear: Saturday (Sabbath) recalled God's day of rest after the work of creation; Sunday (the Lord's day) pointed ahead to the *new* creation of the promised 'new heavens and new earth' (see, for instance, Revelation 21.1), inaugurated by Jesus' resurrection. The idea of Sunday as a Christian day of rest was not developed until the fourth century, when Christianity was in a position of dominance within the Roman empire and Sunday could be made a weekly public holiday. Sunday as a day for gathering and for corporate worship, however, seems to have been an early development.

In fact, the pattern of the weekly remembrance of the resurrection seems to have developed long before the annual celebration of the resurrection at Easter. In this sense Easter is a 'big Sunday' rather than Sunday being a 'mini-Easter'. Even as the Christian year developed in later centuries and began to dominate, Sunday was still seen as essentially a celebration of the resurrection, whatever season of the year it was.

The year: engaging with the gospel message

An annual pattern of Christian celebrations gives us a similar chance to orientate ourselves over a longer period. There are the great Christian festivals of Christmas, Easter and Pentecost, which celebrate the key elements of the life of Christ and the gift of the Spirit. Each developed periods of preparation (Advent and Lent). Of course, there is no absolute reason why the year should be structured in this particular way, but the structuring of time in some sort of way does seem to be a natural human pattern, and it is no surprise that this should be reflected in the corporate worship of the Church.

The peaks

The festivals form the focal or 'high' points through the year. Those that we have inherited were not arrived at in a systematic way, but developed at different times, for different reasons and in different ways.

■ **Easter**, as a Christian observance of the Jewish Passover, was
the first annual festival to develop. The first clear evidence of
it comes from Asia Minor in the second century. At first there
was no 'Holy Week' leading up to Easter Day – just one day of
celebration, which was like Good Friday and Easter Day all rolled
into one. Holy Week (as a sort of 're-enactment' of the events of
the last week of Jesus' life, from Palm Sunday, through Maundy
Thursday, Good Friday and on to Easter Sunday) seems to have
begun in the fourth century, spurred on by the experiences of
pilgrims in Jerusalem itself, where you could walk the actual
route to Calvary, visit the site of the garden tomb, and so on.
As pilgrims returned home Holy Week began to find its way
into the annual pattern of many churches around the world.

The medieval period saw the liturgical celebration of the
events leading up to Easter develop yet further and become
increasingly tied to the historical events and the days on which
they took place. Because of the significance of the Lord's day, as
noted above, the dominant pattern that emerged was for Easter
always to be celebrated on a Sunday, whichever day of the week
the Jewish Passover fell on. However, differences between East
and West in how the date of Easter is calculated mean that
in most years the Christian Church is divided over when it
celebrates Easter.

■ **Pentecost** (from the Greek for 'the fiftieth day') was a Jewish
harvest celebration fifty days after Passover. It acquired new
meaning for Christians after the Holy Spirit was poured out
on the apostles at that festival, and so the Church began to
celebrate the ascension of Jesus and the gift of the Spirit on
the fiftieth day after Easter. In the fourth century the ascension
of Christ began to be celebrated earlier, on the fortieth day, in
keeping with the timetable given in the book of Acts.

■ **Lent**, as a preparation for Easter, was originally a period of final
intensive preparation for candidates for baptism, at a time when
baptisms took place annually at Easter. The idea of a forty-day
period of fasting which mirrored Jesus' time in the desert
(Matthew 4.1-11) seems to have started in Egypt and was
established by the end of the fourth century. It later developed
into a time of discipline and self-examination for all Christians,
not just candidates for baptism.

- **Christmas** (the celebration of the incarnation) was a relatively late arrival: it seems to have been celebrated widely by the fourth century. In the West it got fixed at 25 December and in the East on 6 January. Eventually East and West adopted each other's celebrations. In the West, 25 December became a celebration of the birth of Christ and 6 January became a connected celebration of the revelation of Christ ('Epiphany'), which focused on three themes: the visit of the wise men; Christ's baptism; and the turning of water into wine at the wedding at Cana.

It wasn't until later still that Christmas became particularly associated with the events of Jesus' birth in the realistic way reflected in cribs and nativity plays that are so much part of our own celebration of Christmas. Saint Francis of Assisi (in the thirteenth century) is said to have been the first to make a crib scene as a visual focus for this celebration.

Using colour to reflect the seasons

In many churches and traditions the liturgical festivals and the seasons that accompany them are reflected in worship not only with different words or forms of service but also with ritual, symbol and colour. Colours have been used to designate different seasons and to assist in setting the 'mood'. Just as people tend naturally to 'dress up' or wear their best, or favourite, clothes on special days in their own lives (just think of weddings), so, in the Church, it became natural to decorate the building with the most expensive materials and for leaders to wear the 'best' at the Church's most special times (such as Easter). At other times, by contrast, decoration and clothing were more 'ordinary', and at some points (Lent, for instance) were deliberately downplayed. The actual colours used have varied in different places and at different times. The widespread use of colour in any systematic way does not seem to have taken place much before the twelfth century. The colour of the season might be reflected in the vestments of the clergy, the decoration of the altar/table, any cloths used to decorate the pulpit or lectern, and any banners or hangings. Recently there has been considerable ecumenical convergence around a standard pattern, but other patterns still dominate in other places. The Sarum Use, for instance (the form of service used at Salisbury Cathedral), which dominated in parish churches in England prior to the Reformation, had its own set of colours.

Season	Ecumenical 'Western' colours	Sarum colours
Advent	Purple	Blue
Christmas, Easter	White or gold	White or gold
Lent	Purple, or simple linen	Simple linen
Pentecost, Holy Week and celebrations of saints who were martyred	Red	Gold or white for Pentecost; Black for Holy Week
Ordinary time	Green	Red

One important advantage of some sort of planned progression through the year, during which the key aspects of the Christian faith are encountered, is that it prevents us, or our leaders, from avoiding those parts of the year that are least comfortable. Good Friday is never a particularly easy day to go to church (even if your work patterns allow you to do so) – but it is good that every year the Church is forced to reckon with Jesus' suffering and sense of abandonment, and the cost to him of our salvation.

The plains

Between these peaks there are the plains of what is sometimes called 'ordinary time'. This echoes our own experience of living as Christians and affirms that the ordinary times of our straightforward 'plod with God' are just as important as the mountaintop times when we are especially conscious of God and his work in our lives. The ordinary time helps the peaks to stand out.

The ordinary time is interspersed with other anniversaries and special days, which might celebrate such things as:

■ the birth of a 'saint';

■ the death of a martyr;

- the remembrance of some local Christian hero
(such as Hilda or Cuthbert);

- the anniversary of the dedication of a church building; or

- the anniversary of a significant event in the life of a church's
founder (such as Aldersgate Sunday in the Methodist Church,
which commemorates John Wesley's experience of having his
heart 'strangely warmed').

From circle to spiral

Liturgical worship is sometimes criticized for 'going nowhere'
except round and round in circles, and it is easy to see why worship
which seems to be much the same from one Sunday to the next
could seem to be stuck in a pretty deep rut. But it does not have
to be like that (and ruts are not restricted to services which are
consciously 'liturgical'). There is no reason why using the same
words, or celebrating the same festivals, or doing it in much the
same way, should by definition leave people stuck in a rut. The plays
of Shakespeare have been performed all over the world for some
four hundred years and, though the plot and the dialogue is always
the same, each generation, indeed each director and cast, brings
fresh meaning and emphasis to the same plays.

Whatever the form of service, the people taking part and the world
beyond the Church are changing all the time. The same words are
never heard in exactly the same context. Even within the worship
itself, the accompaniments to the words (action, movement, music,
silence, symbol, etc.) give opportunities for creativity and freshness.
The key to liturgical worship is to ensure that the annual, daily and
weekly cycles do not become a comfortable roundabout, but a
dynamic way of moving people on – not a circle, which returns to
the same point unchanged, but a spiral, which expands as you go
round so that you never return to quite the same spot.

For further reflection...

1. At what part of the day do you find it easiest (and hardest)
    to pray?
2. What are your favourite and least favourite days or seasons
    of the liturgical year, and why?

3.   What are your personal or family anniversaries? Do you have ways of making them part of your prayer and thanksgiving?

4.   In your own pattern of following the Christian year (or that of your church), do you think that there are any aspects of the gospel that get too much or too little attention? How could things be improved?

6

Liturgy and the ordering of the imagination

In Chapter 5 we explored how liturgical worship's strong sense of structure can be applied to the days, weeks and years of our lives so that the very way that we understand our passage through time is shaped by worship. In this chapter we turn our attention to some of the other ways that worship can shape how we make sense of our lives, by painting in our imaginations new ways of understanding the world and our part in it. Because liturgical worship ought to be structured and shaped by history and the wider Church, it can provide something against which to test our individual and localized world-views, so that our imagination is changed. This ability to imagine things being different is at the heart of believing that the reign of God can grow and overcome all that opposes it. In worship it involves doing, saying, thinking and feeling things that sometimes run counter to what we experience in the rest of our lives.

Actions and words

Despite the common association of liturgy with words alone, liturgical worship is shaped as much by actions as by words – and usually by both working together.

Sometimes the wider context makes the meaning clear. A hug or the touch of a hand on a shoulder at a funeral needs no accompanying words of sympathy – the situation makes it obvious what is meant. Similarly, reaching out to touch a cross, or to kiss it, on Good Friday says more than words can. Yet even powerful actions such as these need words and some context in order to gain their meaning, their 'theological shape'. Consider the lighting of a candle. A candle lit at Evening Prayer, accompanied by a prayer thanking God for the light, symbolizes one thing. A candle lit as names of the departed are read out at an annual service of remembrance symbolizes something else; and a candle given to a newly baptized person means something else again. The Eucharist provides the classic example of actions which

are given new meanings by words: 'This is my body', 'Do this
in remembrance'.

Sometimes those words immediately surround the action, making
the meaning and function clear. For instance, as a candle is lit
someone says, 'We light this candle as a sign of our hope in the
light of Christ conquering the darkness.'

Sometimes, the action takes its meaning or meanings from words
which form a much more general context, surrounding the action
but at a greater distance. For instance, someone might read a
passage of Scripture about light and darkness. This might be
followed by a time of silence, and then a song or hymn about
light during which a candle is lit, without further spoken words.

Occasionally words may impose a single meaning on an action;
more often they set a context in which actions can be understood,
while retaining an element of ambiguity or providing for meanings
to be grasped at many different levels.

Similarly, words used in different contexts can carry different
meanings or interpret or subvert the situation. Think of the words
often known as the Nunc Dimittis (the song of Simeon from Luke
2.29-32): 'Now, Lord, you let your servant go in peace...'. In the
context of a service of Evening Prayer they might form a reflection
on the New Testament reading. In the context of a funeral, read
as the coffin is being carried out of church, the words evoke quite
different sentiments and carry different emphases.

Conversely, the context in which words are spoken, or the
accompanying action, can influence the meaning placed upon
the words themselves. Think of a service in which these sentences
were read out, slowly:

> *The world is full of darkness and confusion.*
>
> *The world is full of pain and suffering.*
>
> *The world is full of violence and anger.*

Not particularly good news! But imagine the same words being
spoken and, after each sentence, a candle being lit. In that context
the words do not provide the meaning of the candles: the candles,
bringing light, affect and subvert the meaning of the words. Instead
of bald statements of despair they become descriptions of situations

in which God's light can shine. The darkness of confusion, pain and suffering is put in the bigger context of God's light.

This juxtaposition of words and actions, or words in particular situations, each of which may influence and interpret the other, is one of the basic building blocks of liturgy. Meanings are 'broken' by such juxtapositions, and new meanings and understandings made possible.

Liturgical language

The language used in liturgical worship tends to be richer, more formal and more complex than the language of spontaneous prayer – in much the same way that the language and expression used in songs and hymns is very different from that used in normal conversation, because it is tapping into our imaginations. The richness of liturgical expression is simply the result of someone (or some people) having given time, thought and preparation to the words. It is a particular skill to be able to write words that can bear repetition (sometimes very regular repetition) while remaining fresh. It is a different skill from the ability to pray well spontaneously, and both gifts are vital in the Church.

Liturgical words often have to be spoken by the whole congregation, rather than by a single voice, and forming those sorts of words is also a particular skill. People often suggest that liturgy would be much better if poets were involved in crafting the words, but the skills required by liturgy are not the same as the skills of the poet – though, of course, a particular individual may have both.

Although care needs to be taken that the language used in worship is accessible and understandable (and this is just as important in non-liturgical worship), it is important to remember that understanding depends as much on the context in which words are used as it does on the vocabulary. To understand even the most basic Christian terms (such as 'God', 'grace', 'salvation' and so on) requires exposure to the use of these terms in the story of God's action, as recorded in Scripture and echoed in worship. This is the natural way that language is learnt.

Doing by saying

As well as considering the meaning, it is important to ask, 'What is this language *doing*?' Words perform particular functions in corporate worship. In liturgical worship those functions are usually explicit because the worship has a clear structure and each part has a particular role. Such functions include giving blessings, professing belief, and pronouncing absolutions. The language tends to be very bold: 'The blessing of God almighty . . . be upon you and remain with you'; 'I believe in Jesus Christ, . . . who was conceived by the Holy Spirit'; 'Almighty God . . . have mercy upon you'.

All language functions in different ways in different contexts. So what does the liturgical context do to the things that we say in church? Take the reciting of one of the creeds, for instance. A whole series of overlapping things could be going on. For instance, if the Nicene Creed is recited weekly the words will be the same each week and each worshipper will have the same text in front of them. And yet, according to the context and the people, that same creed may be functioning in a number of different ways:

- as a statement of belief (though there may be different understandings in the minds of different worshippers about what it means that Christ 'was incarnate from the Holy Spirit and the virgin Mary' or 'descended to the dead');

- as an act of praise (there is an unspoken, but clearly intended, assumption that these things we believe are good things, for which it is right to praise God);

- as a personal testimony (this was not my belief three years ago; the fact that I can now say this creed expresses a change in my life);

- as a response to the preaching (credal statements are often placed after the sermon in services, and therefore can function as an explicit response to it);

- as an expression of belonging (in stating this belief we show our connection with the rest of the universal Church).

Some Christians are unhappy with language that works at different levels, performs different functions and does not make straightforward statements. It is sometimes tempting to simplify or clarify. Context is everything, however, and sometimes the search for 'clarity' can undermine both meaning and impact. A phrase like, 'Send down your Holy Spirit upon us', would be open to all sorts of criticisms if it were found in a theological textbook:

- we don't really think that God is 'up there' sending the Spirit *down*;

- we believe that the Spirit is unconstrained and not limited to one place, so doesn't need to be 'sent';

- we believe Christians all have the Holy Spirit anyway, so why ask for more?

- can we really speak so directly to God, as if he were at our beck and call?

- etc., etc.

And yet, in context, the phrase is not only understandable, it is also a good deal more powerful and evocative than any attempt to spell out what is being said in more straightforward terms. Like poetry and jokes, some forms of words in worship lose something when reduced to a straightforward, one-dimensional statement.

Liturgical language recognizes that words and actions do not merely express what we feel or believe; they can express a deeper reality and they can make that reality happen. Hence, to thank God for his love even when you do not *feel* thankful is not hypocrisy but formation: allowing yourself to be shaped by the truth. To exchange vows in a marriage service is not just to express that you wish to be married, it brings about your marriage. Liturgical worship assumes that body, mind and spirit are interconnected, so that it is not just that we express with our bodies or voices what we think in our minds or feel in our hearts: on the contrary, what we do with our bodies or say with our mouths can change or influence how we feel and what we think, as individuals and as communities. Consider this example. In his first letter to the church at Corinth, the apostle Paul wrote:

> *The bread that we break, is it not a sharing in the body of Christ? Because there is one bread, we who are many are one body, for we all partake of the one bread.*

1 Corinthians 10.16-17

In some churches this passage is taken as the basis for words used as the bread is broken at communion. For instance:

> We break this bread
> to share in the body of Christ.
> **Though we are many, we are one body.**
> *because we all share in one bread.*

Common Worship, *Holy Communion Order One [emphasis added]*

Note how Paul puts it. We might have expected him to put it the other way round: 'We who are many partake of the one bread *because* we are one body.' Instead, he says that we are one because we share in one bread. The 'liturgical' action fosters the unity, it doesn't merely express it.

Actions, objects and space

As well as words, the actions of liturgical worship often require objects and some space in which to take place. Sometimes the importance of the action has been almost lost in the concerns about the objects and the spaces. Consider these two examples.

Holy Communion

■ The primary **action** is eating and drinking together in remembrance of Jesus (as he commanded), preceded by giving thanks (as Jesus gave thanks).

■ The **objects** required for this are bread and wine and, secondarily, a plate and a cup in which to hold them.

■ The **space** in which this action takes place is determined by two things: first, by the table (or 'altar') on which the bread and wine are placed for thanksgiving and from which they are shared; and second, by the manner in which they will be shared (for instance, will they be brought to the people or will the people approach the table?).

There will always be discussions about what sort of bread and wine to use (e.g. leavened or unleavened bread? Wafers or a loaf? Alcoholic or non-alcoholic wine?) and what form the cup and plate should take (e.g. silver or pottery? One cup or individual glasses?) and what the altar-table should look like (e.g. rectangular, circular or square? How much like a normal table?) and where it stands (e.g. in the centre or against a wall?). These, however, must all serve the primary symbolic action of everyone sharing bread and wine, as equals before God.

Reading from Scripture

- The **actions** are proclaiming, hearing and responding to God's word. Any congregational response (such as, 'This is the word of the Lord – Thanks be to God') is about the proclamation, not about the book.

- The **object** required is a book, or some other means of providing the words of Scripture.

- The **space** in which this action takes place may be determined by a stand on which to place the book (a 'lectern') and there may be other requirements to ensure that the reader can be seen and heard.

   For the proclamation to be seen, heard and recognized as important it might be appropriate to use a large Bible, read from a raised platform, use a microphone, or form a procession to a suitable place – but these things must serve, and not *determine*, the action. For instance, if a 'gospel procession' to the centre of the church means that the reader cannot be heard because there is no microphone available there, then the procession has undermined the importance of the gospel reading, not enhanced it.

The objects used in worship, the particular places where actions happen, and the whole space in which the worship takes place, should all relate back to the basic liturgical actions they are designed to support and facilitate. For instance, church buildings with long naves and rows of seats facing the same way can signal strongly that we are all 'heading in the same direction'. With a focus that is before and ahead of us they can give a sense of the glory and transcendence of God. They also make processions and movement to the front straightforward. Sharing the peace, however, is made more clumsy by such an arrangement, and a font placed in the back corner of such a church can appear marginalized – 'out of sight, out of mind' – even if the intention was to place it near the main door as a sign that baptism is the 'way in'.

On the other hand, a worship space arranged in a circle or ellipse makes it easy to be aware of other people and to engage them in eye contact. Sharing the peace in that context feels very natural. However, the inward focus can hinder us from looking beyond one another to God or to the world.

Music and singing

Songs, hymns and anthems have the ability to combine intellectual content with emotional impact: this is what makes music so powerful in worship. Singing is so closely associated with Christian worship that it is often tempting to see the two as the same. In fact singing, and the use of music, has been controversial at different times in the history of the Church. Worship in the synagogue probably included simple unaccompanied singing, and many of the early Christian writers encouraged this in order that the emphasis should be on the words. They did not want the words to be swamped or even subverted by the use of instruments. For some Christians the use of musical instruments was too close to the pagan forms of worship.

Today, music is used in different ways in different churches. In Free Churches the congregational singing of hymns has been an important part of their history and originally distinguished them from the Church of England; the hymns can form the main building blocks of the service, along with the readings and sermon. Any spoken prayers or responsive texts are fitted in around them.

In a more liturgical context the spoken (or sung) words of the liturgy are the fixed points and the hymns or songs can be fitted in between them.

In both of these models the songs, like the readings or the prayers, are simply further elements to be slotted in.

A different way of using music is to see it not as a separate element but as a tool to be used with other elements. Music can then be used in different ways:

- it can set a mood;

- it can provide space for reflection;

- it can highlight key parts of the service;

- it can echo and reinforce other elements of the service.

Using music as a tool means using it to emphasize the readings or the communion; it means allowing it to move us during our prayers; it means using it to aid reflection and response after the sermon. In this way, music contributes to the shaping of the act of worship and the shaping of our hearts through worship.

In some traditions this is achieved by setting the words of liturgical texts themselves to music so that they can be sung, not just said. At the other end of the spectrum there may be no liturgical texts at all and songs and hymns may have to do the work of structuring the act of worship on their own. Both are examples of music being used to shape the worship, rather than being merely one element of it.

Movement

The 1970s and 1980s saw a revival of interest in the role of dance in liturgical worship. 'Liturgical dance' groups were formed and in some churches it is still an important aspect of worship. Though liturgical dance does not now seem so fashionable, this is not because the movement has proved to be unimportant, but because some of the foundational principles have now been accepted and found other expression. The idea that we need to express our worship with our emotions and our bodies, as well as our minds, has gained wide acceptance. Churches of all traditions are now much more likely to move around the building during worship (for instance, gathering at the font for a baptism, rather than merely turning towards it). The list of 'acceptable' physical expressions in worship has grown in most churches. Previously, it might only have included sitting, standing and kneeling. Now it might include clapping, swaying, raising arms in praise, waving flags or streamers, dancing, and even prostrating oneself on the floor. The sharing of the peace, in even the most formal of contexts, has added to worship itself the experience of moving around, greeting people, shaking hands (and sometimes exchanging hugs), rather than restricting it to the fellowship after the service is over.

Deliberately engaging our bodies in worship gives shape to important Christian doctrines. The goodness of the physical creation (though spoiled by sin), the image of God in humankind (though marred by sin) and the reality of the incarnation are beliefs that are belied by merely cerebral worship.

A sense of the liturgical adds a corporate dimension to this physical expression in worship. The structure of liturgical worship and the sense of 'given' movements (rather than only spontaneous ones) reminds us that physical expression needs to go beyond the individual level to express something of our belonging together in worship. It is good, for instance, to be invited to 'sit or stand as you find most comfortable' during periods of singing: but it can also be good to stand *together*, or to form a procession *together*, or to come forward *together* to receive communion.

The senses in worship

We have already considered the importance of action, movement and the things that we say, sing and hear in worship. What about sight and smell?

As with music, the Church has wrestled with the issue of visual images and stimuli in worship. At the Reformation, much of the visual stimulus of medieval church buildings such as statues, wall paintings and stained glass was removed. The aim was to focus attention on hearing and understanding, so that the congregation could take a greater part. There was a parallel fear that 'images' could be distracting, misunderstood and used in superstitious ways. From a different perspective, the ikons of the Eastern churches are seen as doorways into a fuller spiritual reality, that can only deepen the experience of worship. The rich decoration and use of imagery in Orthodox church buildings is intended, in a similar way, to capture something of the heavenly reality here on earth.

No matter how stimulating the sermon or the prayers or the songs, eyes wander. What do they see? Crosses? Banners? Words written on walls? A table? An altar? Elaborate decoration? Peeling paint and crumbling plaster? Pictures in stained glass? The world outside through plain glass? From whichever perspective we come, it is clear that what the eyes encounter when corporate worship takes place will have some considerable impact on our imaginations.

In some traditions incense is used to provide an ambient smell to worship. Incense speaks both of prayer (Psalm 141.2; Revelation 5.8) and of 'specialness'. It combines smell and sight and, in a culture where aromatherapy is very popular, it is perhaps time for us to discover afresh how our understanding of God can be 'formed and shaped' by what we smell when we gather for worship.

Sight, sound, shape, action – even smell – are part of corporate worship in any tradition, whether attention is given to them or not. Worship that is liturgical will see these things as 'tools', given by God to be used in the structuring of worship so that it engages with us as whole beings: body, mind and spirit.

For further reflection...

1. Consider the ways that music is used in the worship in your church. Is music used as one element of the worship, or as a tool to enhance all elements?

2. Do you think there is enough silence in your worship? If not, at which points would you appreciate more?

3. What is the main and most obvious visual focus in the room in which your church worships? What effect do you think it has on the assumptions of regular worshippers and what might it say to visitors?

4. Which senses are primarily engaged in the worship in your church, and in what ways?

7

Elements of liturgical worship 1: some basics

We have seen that liturgy is the public, symbolic shaping of space and time in order that our hearts and lives might be shaped in the image of Christ. In this chapter we are going to consider some of the key elements of liturgical worship in general, and how they form 'patterns' – patterns that, in turn, form us. We shall turn to the elements that are particular to the Eucharist in Chapter 8.

A worship checklist

Any church can develop a checklist of 'must-have' elements in worship. Such a list might include:

- Praise

- Thanksgiving

- Confession

- Prayers

- Bible reading

- Preaching

In addition, there are other things to keep an eye on:

- Is there some solid doctrinal content?

- Is there opportunity for worshippers' emotions to be engaged and feelings to be expressed?

- Is there a proper balance in the use of different parts of the Bible (for instance, is the sermon always based on the Gospel reading)?

Liturgical worship simply allows this checklist to be determined in conversation with the wider Church (see 'Where are decisions taken?', page 22). Sometimes it means submitting local decisions to the authority of the wider Church. The checklist is tighter in some circumstances than in others (for instance, most churches tend to have stricter rules about Holy Communion than non-eucharistic services, and the rules about marriage services tend to be very tight because of the legal implications). The more formally 'liturgical' the church is, the more likely the checklist is to include not only types of material (such as 'intercessions') but actual forms of words (such as the Lord's Prayer or the Nicene Creed).

Whether you call it 'liturgy' or not, the checklist is intended in all cases to protect the worshippers by ensuring that important things are not forgotten, that less important things are not over-emphasized and that the fullness of the gospel is engaged with over time.

So let's work through a typical service, considering some of the elements that might be encountered and what they 'do' liturgically. These could include:

- Gathering

- Confessing sin and being assured of forgiveness

- Reading and responding to Scripture

- Affirming our faith

- Praying

- Being sent out.

Gathering

In different churches and at various services you may find the first part of a service called different things: Gathering; Preparation; Call to Worship. Each has a slightly different emphasis but the basic idea which is being given 'shape' is the same: though God graciously allows us access into his presence, we do not presume upon that access, charging in without considering who it is that we come to worship.

Call it 'Gathering', and you stress the importance of the individuals who have come together, expressing the belief that they are part of the body of Christ and that their worship will be inherently corporate and not merely collective.

Call it 'Preparation', and you stress the importance of being ready to encounter God in a focused way and to hear God's word and respond to it.

Describe it as 'Call to Worship', and you reflect the reality that, in our lives as well as at church, worship is not just a luxury to be chosen, or not, as the whim takes us. Rather, worship is part of our calling, and just as the psalms often do, we encourage one another to it (and indeed, sometimes encourage ourselves, as we speak directly to our own hearts).

Confession

An element of penitence, often formalized in a confession and an absolution (or 'declaration of God's forgiveness' by a minister) is a common part of most liturgical worship. There is no direct evidence in the New Testament that it was part of the gatherings for praise and prayer, though there is the injunction to 'confess your sins to one another' (James 5.16). In the earliest account of a eucharist that we have outside the New Testament (Justin Martyr's account from around AD 150 – see Chapter 4, pp. 46–7) it is not mentioned specifically, though it could have been a part of the prayers.

The act of repentance finds a regular place in worship simply because it is such a core aspect of the Christian faith. The call to be baptized is a call to 'repent and believe' and it was the regular call of Jesus to those who wanted to follow him. But repentance is not a one-off act, it is a way of life – a continual turning towards God and away from all that competes with God in our lives. Hence, in public worship penitence (and some assurance of God's forgiveness – for the one without the other is only half the Christian story) is a natural symbolic expression of the constant call to repent and believe, and points us back to our baptism, at which we signed up (or were signed up by our parents) for such a way of life.

The different ways that penitence is expressed and the different points at which it takes place can give 'shape' to different truths. For many the natural place for penitence is near the start of the service – clearing the way, as it were, before reaching the heart of the act of worship. In this position it gives shape to the fact that grace, though free 'at the point of need', is not 'cheap'; though we come freely into God's presence, we do not do so arrogantly or taking God for granted.

It can be equally valid to delay any confession to later in the service. This allows the opening part of the service to express the grace of God in a more unqualified way and gives shape to the fact that grace precedes our response to God and is not dependent on it: God cannot be 'bought'. Penitence might then be used as part of the response to the readings and the preaching, or as part of the prayers.

The giving of some form of 'absolution' by an ordained priest or minister is not universal (and some churches deliberately avoid it), but reassuring God's people of God's love and forgiveness is important for all.

In the Church of England there are a number of authorized forms of absolution, including this one from *Common Worship*:

> Almighty God, who forgives all who truly repent,
> have mercy upon you,
> pardon and deliver you from all your sins,
> confirm and strengthen you in all goodness,
> and keep you in life eternal,
> through Jesus Christ our Lord.
> **Amen.**

A prayer like this is written very carefully to ensure that it gives a confident declaration of God's forgiveness, while making clear that the authority to do so comes from God and that repentance is the appropriate response to God's grace.

The *Methodist Worship Book* often concludes confession with words such as these:

> Christ Jesus came into the world to save sinners.
> This is his gracious word:
> 'Your sins are forgiven.'
> **Amen. Thanks be to God.**

Here the emphasis is on God and not the particular minister and the tone is one of joyful assurance of forgiveness, to avoid any suggestion that it might be withheld.

Some churches restrict the giving of an 'absolution' in the 'you' form ('Almighty God . . . have mercy on you') to those who are ordained as priests. This gives shape to a particular view of ordination and priesthood, one which gives the priest the authority to speak in the name of the Church, and in the name of God, in certain contexts. In a church in which those who are not ordained can use a similar form, the 'liturgy' will give shape to a different understanding of how the authority to speak for God works in the Church.

Scripture

Since the early days of the Church, Christians have been reading the Scriptures in public when they meet to worship. First they read the Hebrew Scriptures (what Christians came to call the 'Old Testament'); later they added to these the letters of the apostles and the first written accounts of the life of Jesus – the epistles and Gospels.

It seems that Christians followed the synagogue pattern, reading special passages to suit the time of year around the festivals, and the rest of the time working through the Scriptures passage by passage.

There is no single way of ordering the public reading of the Bible. Different churches at different times have come up with their own 'lectionary' – a list of passages to be read on given days.

Today there are many different lectionary patterns. A common ecumenical choice at the moment is the 1992 *Revised Common Lectionary*. This is a three-year cycle of Bible readings, based originally on the three-year *Lectionary for Mass* of the Roman Catholic Church. It has been approved, adopted or adapted by many churches, including the Methodist Church, the United Reformed Church and the Church of England. Each year of the three-year cycle majors on one of the first three Gospels – Matthew, Mark and Luke. John's Gospel features in every year, particularly in the periods before and after Easter.

Denominations differ in their use of the Bible. In some churches the choice of Bible reading is left entirely up to the leader or preacher at a given service. At the other end of the spectrum are churches in which the use of a particular lectionary is compulsory. Others lie somewhere in between these two extremes.

Ladder or scaffolding?

Using a lectionary to control the reading of the Bible in worship is like using scaffolding to paint the outside of your house. Putting the scaffolding together is a time-consuming and skilled task, but once it is done it allows easy access to all parts of the house, allowing for a thorough job.

The alternative is to use a ladder and move it around. In the short term this is much easier and gives good access to some parts of the house. But other parts will be just out of reach, and the temptation will always be to give them cursory attention with the paintbrush and concentrate on the parts that are easy to reach, in order to avoid moving the ladder too many times. Without a lectionary (or some other long-term plan for Bible reading) there is always a risk that preachers or leaders will drift towards the passages that they find congenial or easy to preach on, and avoid those passages that look less promising or which seem to teach something different from to their own views.

On the other hand, if you just want to touch up the paintwork, erecting scaffolding feels like taking a hammer to crack a nut.

No single lectionary or pattern of readings covers the whole Bible in equal depth and all lectionaries have their weaknesses. But some sort of order to the reading of Scripture in public worship, coupled with the use of the Christian year, is one way of avoiding getting stuck on the same old bits of the Bible and the same old aspects of the gospel.

In many churches some sort of formal, congregational response is used when a reading is introduced or concluded. These indicate something of what the Church thinks is happening when Scripture is read. For example:

Before a Gospel reading at Holy Communion:

Hear the Gospel of our Lord Jesus Christ according
to Mark [or Matthew, Luke or John]
Glory to you, O Lord.

After the Gospel reading:

This is the Gospel of the Lord.
Praise to you, O Christ.

A response that may be used after any Bible reading:

This is the word of the Lord.
Thanks be to God.

Church of England, Common Worship

The reader says:

Listen for the word of God.
The reading comes from [book, chapter and verse]

At the end of the reading the reader says:

May God bless to us the reading of his holy Word.
Amen.

Church of Scotland, Book of Common Order, *First Order for Evening Service*

[After the reading] The reader may say:

Hear what the Spirit is saying to the Church.
Thanks be to God.

Anglican Church of Aotearoa, New Zealand and Polynesia A New Zealand
Prayer Book - He Karikia Mihinare O Aotearoa

The writers of Scripture expected their words to be encountered in
this public context of being read aloud. No one in the first century
envisaged a situation where someone would have a personal copy
of the Bible and read it alone. Encountering Scripture by *hearing* it
is inherently corporate: there have to be at least two people – one to
speak and one to hear. Many Bible passages only make proper sense
when that corporate context is understood. For instance, the rather
curious 'let the reader understand' in Mark 13.14 is a direction to
the person reading out loud – the 'abomination of desolation' is code
which needs to be interpreted. Similarly the blessing on 'the one who
reads the words of this prophecy and those who hear it' (Revelation 1.3)

only makes sense in the context of public proclamation rather than private study.

Today most of us are more used to encountering Scripture by seeing it in the printed Bible. The positive side of this is that Scripture can be studied and read by all (or, at least, by all who can read – which does not, of course, mean everybody). The negative side is that Scripture is privatized; we feel we own it as individuals rather than as part of God's people. Hearing God's word regularly read aloud when we gather ought to 'shape' us so that we see it as belonging to us all, together (rather than being our individual property) and intended to be proclaimed (rather than simply read in private).

Affirmations of faith

The most obvious and common affirmations of faith in liturgical worship are the creeds – usually the Apostles' Creed and the Nicene Creed.

Creeds seem to have originated in the context of baptism. These statements of faith made it clear just what the candidate was being baptized 'into'. The earliest and simplest seems to have been 'Jesus is Lord' (Romans 10.9 and 1 Corinthians 12.3). The Apostles' Creed was the first expanded form to emerge. Despite its name it was not written by the apostles, but was clearly thought to be in line with their teaching. It is still widely used as a statement of belief at baptism around the world and across the denominations.

The Nicene Creed is more accurately called the Niceno-Constantinopolitan Creed (you can see why most service books just put 'Nicene'!). It emerged at a time of doctrinal dispute in the Church about the nature of Christ and of God. A draft was produced by church leaders meeting at the Council of Nicaea (in modern-day Turkey) in AD 325 and a modified version was produced by a subsequent council at Constantinople in AD 381. Like the Apostles' Creed, it was originally used in worship in the context of baptism services (in the church in Jerusalem). The first evidence we have for its use in the Eucharist, where it is now most commonly encountered in most churches, dates from the late fifth century (in Antioch).

These two creeds are often called the 'ecumenical' creeds because they were formulated before the split between the Eastern and Western churches in 1054 and because they are widely accepted and used across the churches today. Even so there is still room for dispute. The Eastern churches use the original version of the Nicene Creed without the so-called 'filioque' (Latin for 'and the son') clause. This refers to the line about the Holy Spirit:

who proceeds from the Father [and the Son].

The part in brackets (the *filioque* clause) was added by the Western Church in the sixth century.

Now that modern eucharistic prayers include so much of the story of creation and redemption, some people are calling for the creeds to be used less often, lest they overbalance services of Holy Communion with repeated doctrinal content. Some Churches now allow for alternatives, which are derived from what appear to be affirmations of faith or belief in the Bible. For instance:

Let us affirm our faith in Jesus Christ the Son of God.

Though he was divine,
he did not cling to equality with God,
but made himself nothing.
Taking the form of a slave,
he was born in human likeness.
He humbled himself
and was obedient to death,
even the death of the cross.
Therefore God has raised him on high,
and given him the name above every name:
that at the name of Jesus
every knee should bow,
and every voice proclaim that Jesus Christ is Lord,
to the glory of God the Father.
Amen.

Common Worship, *from Philippians 2.6-11*

Like the ecumenical creeds, these affirmations of faith, coming as they do from the Bible, reflect beliefs that are shared by Christians the world over. They give shape to the idea that the Christian faith is not something that belongs to us alone, nor are we at liberty to change core beliefs about Christ or God on our own. The creeds and scriptural affirmations connect us to the Church in every place and to the Church in different periods of time. Though certain songs or hymns may contain and express doctrinal truths, they do not carry with them the authority that comes from words that have been accepted by Christians around the world and over many centuries.

Prayers

Paul wrote to Timothy:

> *First of all, then, I urge that supplications, prayers,*
> *intercessions, and thanksgivings be made for everyone,*
> *for kings and all who are in high positions, so that we may*
> *lead a quiet and peaceable life in all godliness and dignity.*

1 Timothy 2.1

Churches have been trying to follow this injunction ever since.

Prayer was a natural part of Jewish home life as well as synagogue worship, and it seems likely that this was a normal part of the gatherings of the first Christians. By the time the first accounts of Christian worship were written the 'prayers of the people' were a key part.

Posture for prayer

For the first Christians the normal posture for prayer, at least for the main Sunday gatherings, was standing – a powerful symbol of the confidence of God's people in the presence of their heavenly Father. Kneeling for prayer was common on days other than Sundays and has a long history in England, but it only became the dominant posture (even on Sundays) when God became portrayed as a heavenly version of the earthly rulers (as in the Roman empire after the fourth century and in medieval Europe). Christians then began to behave in God's presence much as they would in the presence of their rulers. The 'hands together' position developed in a similar way: it was normal to show allegiance and submission to a king by adopting this position in his presence.

'Collect' prayers

The 'Collect' (from a Latin word meaning 'assembly') is a particular form of prayer whose origins go back to at least the fifth century in the Western Church. What makes the Collect distinctive is its shape:

Elements of a Collect	Example (*Common Worship*, Collect for the Third Sunday of Easter)
An **address** to God.	*Almighty Father,*
A **truth** about God, which may be the basis for asking	*who in your great mercy gladdened the disciples with the sight of the risen Lord:*
A **request**, sometimes based on this truth.	*give us such knowledge of his presence with us,*
[Sometimes the **purpose** of that request is spelt out.]	*that we may be strengthened and sustained by his risen life and serve you continually in righteousness and truth;*
The **conclusion**, giving the authority for asking, and possibly concluding with a trinitarian formula	*through Jesus Christ your Son our Lord, who is alive and reigns with you, in the unity of the Holy Spirit, one God, now and for ever.*

In a modern Church of England Eucharist the Collect normally comes near the beginning and concludes the Gathering part of the service ('collecting' up the individual prayers of those who have gathered and symbolically offering one prayer to encompass them all, led by the president). Because of its position at the turning point from gathering to giving attention to the Scriptures, the Collect is sometimes treated as a sort of 'theme prayer', introducing in prayer some of the ideas from the Scripture passages.

In non-eucharistic worship the Collect is likely to be part of the main section of prayers, sometimes coming at the end to 'collect up' the preceding prayers.

Prayers of intercession

The Church of England's *Common Worship* service of Holy
Communion Order One gives the following areas that should
be covered in the Prayers of Intercession:

> *The prayers usually include these concerns and may follow
> this sequence:*
>
> ■   *The Church of Christ*
>
> ■   *Creation, human society, the Sovereign and those
>   in authority*
>
> ■   *The local community*
>
> ■   *Those who suffer*
>
> ■   *The communion of saints*

In other churches which give directions, or provide particular forms
of prayer, the list tends to be similar.

Formal periods of prayer may also include penitence (if it does
not feature as a separate section or in the preparation part of the
service) and often include the Lord's Prayer.

The Lord's Prayer

The Lord's Prayer (sometimes called the 'Our Father') is the only form
of prayer which is recorded as having come from the lips of Jesus
himself. However, it is very difficult to know what we should do with
it. In Matthew's account Jesus says, 'Pray then *in this way*' and in
Luke's he says, 'When you pray, *say*'. Christians have differing views
as to whether Jesus intended simply to give us a basic pattern for
prayer or some actual words that we could use. Even if he did think
that we would use his words, it is very difficult to know exactly what
to say (see Chapter 1, page 6)!

In England there are currently three major contenders for a version of the Lord's Prayer which we could share in common:

'Modified traditional' version	International ecumenical modern version	Church of England modern version
Our Father, who art in heaven,	Our Father in heaven,	Our Father in heaven,
hallowed be thy name	hallowed be your name,	hallowed be your name,
thy kingdom come	your kingdom come,	your kingdom come,
thy will be done	your will be done,	your will be done,
on earth as it is in heaven	on earth as in heaven.	on earth as in heaven.
Give us this day our daily bread	Give us today our daily bread.	Give us today our daily bread.
and forgive us our trespasses	Forgive us our sins	Forgive us our sins
as we forgive those who trespass against us	as we forgive those who sin against us.	as we forgive those who sin against us.
And lead us not into temptation	Save us from the time of trial	Lead us not into temptation
but deliver us from evil	and deliver us from evil.	but deliver us from evil.
For thine is the kingdom, the power and the glory, for ever and ever. Amen.	For the kingdom, the power, and the glory are yours, now and forever. Amen.	For the kingdom, the power, and the glory are yours, now and forever. Amen.
This is an adaptation of the version in the Church of England's *Book of Common Prayer* (which has 'Our Father *which* art...' and 'as we forgive *them that* trespass...').	This version was produced by ELLC (English Language Liturgical Consultation), an international ecumenical group which provides modern language versions of many of the texts that are shared across the denominations (such as prayers, creeds and canticles).	This is a variant of the ELLC version, used in the Church of England.

You only have to cross the border from England into Scotland to discover yet another version, which has, 'Forgive us our debts as we forgive our debtors' (see, for instance, the Church of Scotland's *Book of Common Order*).

The final part of the prayer ('For the kingdom, the power and the glory' – usually called the 'doxology') is not included in the words that Jesus gave us. It began to be added to the version of the prayer in manuscripts of Matthew's Gospel some time in the fourth century – probably an example of liturgical use affecting the version recorded in the evolving Scriptures. We are not certain why it began to be added, but it was probably due to the normal Jewish practice of ending all prayers with a doxology – an ascription of praise to God. The New Testament includes many such doxologies (such as 1 Peter 4.11 – which is similar to the doxology added to the Lord's Prayer) and it may be that when the Lord's Prayer began to be used in worship it became normal, at least in some places, to add a doxology to it.

Throughout Christian history the use of the doxology with the Lord's Prayer has varied:

- The Greek Orthodox Church has, from as early as we know, included the doxology as an integral part of the prayer.

- Many other Eastern churches finish the prayer like this: 'deliver us from evil', followed by a short prayer for deliverance from evil said by the priest, then the doxology is added. This is the pattern now followed in the Roman Catholic Mass.

- In the Roman Catholic Church the doxology was not included at all until the revised translations of the Mass in 1970. When it is used in other forms of service the prayer still ends after 'deliver us from evil'.

- Many of the Western churches that emerged out of the sixteenth-century Reformation began to include the doxology as an integral part of the prayer.

- In the Church of England's *Book of Common Prayer* the Lord's Prayer occurs twice in both Morning and Evening Prayer and in the service of Holy Communion – in each case once with the doxology and once without it!

Being sent out

If the Gathering at the beginning of the service is a vital element, symbolizing our calling to be gathered into the body of Christ, and facilitating that sense of being part of the body in the particular act of worship, then the 'sending out' at the other end of the service is equally important.

Again, terminology varies (Conclusion; Dismissal; Sending Out, etc.) but most modern liturgies are united in giving proper attention to how the service ends, so that worshippers do not simply stop but are sent. Symbolically this is important. Christians are not only called but 'sent': to live lives which glorify God, to make more disciples of Christ and to bear witness to God's action in our lives. The growing consciousness in northern Europe of being a Church in 'mission mode' (even in countries which have traditionally seen themselves as 'Christian') has affected how this part of worship is seen. Going out into the world is where worship meets mission head on. In many contexts the worshippers are only being sent out to coffee in a neighbouring hall, but this is still the beginning of the application of what we have said and sung to the ordinary business of chatting, meeting new people, spilling drinks, sharing news, disciplining children, and so on.

Sometimes the end of a service includes a specific prayer about going out and getting on with it, like this one from the Church of England's *Common Worship* Holy Communion Order One, which specifically connects the act of receiving Holy Communion with the call to live out what the Eucharist means:

> **Almighty God,**
> **we thank you for feeding us**
> **with the body and blood of your Son Jesus Christ.**
> **Through him we offer you our souls and bodies**
> **to be a living sacrifice.**
> **Send us out**
> **in the power of your Spirit**
> **to live and work**
> **to your praise and glory.**
> **Amen.**

Other common elements at the end of a service include a prayer of blessing (referred to as the Benediction in some traditions), the Grace, or some other more general prayer for God to be with us.

Services of all sorts increasingly finish with a final 'off you go', which may come after the blessing. Often it takes this sort of form:

> Go in peace to love and serve the Lord.
> **In the name of Christ. Amen.**
>
> *(or)*
>
> Go in the peace of Christ.
> **Thanks be to God.**

You can't get much clearer than that in showing that worship is meant to send us out for service, not shelter us from unwelcome reality.

The Eucharist

In some traditions the norm would be for a main weekly act of worship (and sometimes daily acts of worship) to include the Eucharist. In other traditions the Eucharist is shared less frequently, either out of a sense of how special it is, or out of a desire to make it easier for visitors who are unfamiliar with Holy Communion to feel comfortable. Whether it happens often or rarely, if it is part of the service it is a major element, and so we have given a whole chapter, Chapter 8, to consider the elements specific to the Eucharist.

For further reflection…

1. Can you think of other elements that you feel should be part of regular public worship? Why do you think they are so important?

2. Are any of the elements mentioned in this chapter absent from the worship in your church? If so, why do you think that is?

8

Elements of liturgical worship 2: the Eucharist

In this chapter we are focusing on those elements which are *particular* to the Eucharist. In addition to those things we consider below, the elements mentioned in the previous chapter will, of course, be just as important in a eucharist as they are in a non-eucharistic act of worship.

The structure of the Eucharist

It is possible to see the Eucharist as basically a two-part service: Word (which includes readings, sermon and prayers) and Sacrament (the thanksgiving over bread and wine and their distribution to the people). In the fourth century the divide between the two was quite clear, because those who were preparing for Christian initiation (the 'catechumens') were dismissed after the first part of the service (just after the prayers). The second part, the 'holy mysteries', were seen as suitable only for those who had committed themselves to Christ in baptism. This fits neatly with a theory (and it is only a theory) that the first 'Word' part of the service derives from the synagogue model and the second part from the meals in which the Lord's Supper was first shared.

The peace

The 'kiss of peace' seems to have been an integral part of the life and worship of the New Testament Church. Many of Paul's letters conclude with the exhortation to 'greet one another with a holy kiss' (for example, Romans 16.16; 1 Corinthians 16.20; 2 Corinthians 13.12) and Peter urges his readers to 'Greet one another with a kiss of love' (1 Peter 5.14). This practice of men and women kissing one another (no formal handshakes in the early years) was a scandal and shock to those outside the Church in the Roman world, for whom kissing was reserved for the closest members of one's family. This was exactly the point: Christians saw themselves as radically connected to one another within the body of Christ, adopted as sons and daughters in God's family. The kiss of peace was a radical and subversive prophetic action in a world where relationships were tightly controlled and defined. It is interesting that in many parts of the Church today, the peace is strongly resisted. Many see the business of moving about to greet one another in the Lord's name with his peace (even if it is restricted to a simple handshake) as inappropriate and irreverent in the midst of worship. It is seen as a distraction and a disruption of worship rather than a crucial aspect of the kingdom of God breaking into our worship. This is understandable. Justin mentions it in his accounts in the second century but it very soon got lost, reduced to a mere token exchange between the clergy and then disappearing altogether in many churches. It was only recovered in the latter half of the twentieth century in most churches, and is therefore seen as an innovation and, like most innovations, resisted.

In many churches the peace acts as a hinge point between the Word part of the service and the Sacrament part. In the Roman Catholic Church the peace comes later, just before the reception of communion, where it acts as a reinforcement of the sense of being in 'holy fellowship' (which is what holy communion means).

The peace is gradually being discovered as a liturgical element in its own right, not only appropriate for Holy Communion services. It is a regular feature of non-eucharistic worship in some churches. It is increasingly seen as giving shape to a truth that we need to live out – the essentially corporate nature of being 'in Christ' and the importance of being in right relationships with one another as well as with God.

Giving shape to the eucharistic action

One of the key differences between the Last Supper and most celebrations of the Eucharist today is that the Last Supper really was a supper, and the sharing of the bread was separated from the sharing of the wine by the intervening parts of the meal. From the New Testament accounts, it is possible to isolate the actions which Jesus performed (seven of them), and recent revision of the Eucharist in most churches has sought to make these actions clearer. In the process of being separated from the context of a meal, the seven actions of Jesus became four actions in our services.

The seven actions of Jesus at the Last Supper

1.	Took bread.
2.	Gave thanks over the bread.
3.	Broke the bread.
4.	Shared the bread.

Other parts of the meal.

5.	Took the cup of wine.
6.	Gave thanks over the wine.
7.	Shared the wine.

The four basic actions, without the meal	The equivalent action in the Eucharist today
1. Take the bread and wine.	Make things ready practically: prepare the table and the bread and wine. In some churches the bread and wine are symbolically 'taken' into the hands of the presiding minister and placed back on the table.
2. Give thanks over the bread and wine.	Say or sing the Eucharistic Prayer – the prayer of thanksgiving.
3. Break the bread.	Break the bread – often with accompanying words.
4. Share the bread and wine.	Share the bread and wine. In some churches it is passed from person to person; in others it is distributed by the minister(s), sometimes assisted by other people.

Preparing the bread and wine

We begin with the first of the four actions. In origin this was simply the practical action of Jesus taking the bread and wine into his hands in order to give thanks over them (and, in the case of the bread, to break it) and then to pass it on to his disciples. In Justin's account he mentions that the bread and wine were brought to the president ready for him to give thanks over them.

In many Churches this practical action never developed beyond whatever was necessary to make the bread and wine ready for the prayer of thanksgiving. By contrast, in the medieval Church this part of the service (called in Latin the *offertorium*, from which we get 'offertory') developed some very elaborate ritual.

In the first half of the twentieth century the new emphasis on shape, with the 'taking' as the first of the four actions, allowed the 'offertory' to grow, even in those churches where previously it was hardly noticed. Offertory processions became popular, with lay people bringing forward the bread and wine. Offertory prayers became commonplace, such as, 'Blessed are you, Lord our God, king of the universe, through your goodness we have this bread to offer/share, fruit of the earth and work of human hands...'. All this resonated with the growing desire to connect Sunday worship with the world of work. Here was a way of offering to God all that we are and do (symbolized by the bread and wine – combining God's provision with human labour) in order for him to transform it and give it back to us as (or symbolizing) the body and blood of Christ. If you take the collection of money at the same time, as many churches do, then this double 'offering' of money along with bread and wine, as symbols of what we bring to God, begins to look like a very significant liturgical moment. If, on the other hand, you take the collection of money after communion, then the dynamic which is being given a liturgical 'shape' is very different: our offering of money (symbolizing all that we offer to God) becomes a response to what he has done for us in Christ. In that case, the bringing of bread and wine to the table may be seen as a complementary, but preliminary, 'offering', or it may become a primarily practical action again.

'Altar' or 'table'?

We saw in Chapter 1 that the early Christians were conscious of not having sacrifices, priests or temples, all of which were fulfilled in Jesus and the Church. Yet it was not long before Christians needed to defend themselves against the accusation that they were atheists (on the grounds that they didn't have all the things that 'normal' religions did, like sacrifices, priests and temples). They began to say things like, 'Well, we don't have sacrifices, but we do have something like it, which uses bread and wine and reminds us of an ultimate sacrifice. And though we don't have priests, we have people who are in charge at this bread and wine action: they are our equivalent to priests.'

In time the language of priests and sacrifices was applied to Christian leaders and the Eucharist. In this context it is not surprising that the table on which the bread and wine were placed began to be referred to as the 'altar'. It was the place where the sacrifice of Christ was brought into the present.

Today the Church is split. There are those who most naturally refer to an altar (and in colloquial use we still talk of 'going to the altar' to get married). They may see the Eucharist as primarily a way provided by God for bringing the sacrifice of Christ into connection with us. It is an altar in the sense that it is the place where his sacrifice of long ago is made real to us today.

For others, this is confusing the symbol with the reality. They prefer to talk of the table (perhaps the 'holy table' or 'communion table'). They see the Eucharist as primarily about a meal in which we share, which is most naturally celebrated around a table.

The Eucharistic Prayer

This is the second of the four actions – the giving thanks. Historically the prayer of thanksgiving has been thought of (and often referred to) as the 'consecration' prayer, and some still call it this. The modern trend is to call it the Eucharistic Prayer (or sometimes the Thanksgiving Prayer, or the Great Thanksgiving Prayer). As 'eucharist' means thanksgiving, this title describes most accurately what it is and takes us back to early terminology, before the controversies over what consecration does (or does not) do to bread and wine. It reminds us that, at root, the Eucharistic Prayer is a 'grace' before a meal.

That sense of Jesus being 'here' which we noted earlier is still closely associated with the Eucharist. Christ promised his special presence whenever two or three gathered in his name. In some parts of the Church this focusing of the presence of Christ has come to be especially associated with the service of Holy Communion (and for some, particularly focused in the bread and wine themselves).

Over the centuries there has been much controversy over two key questions about what happens at the Eucharist:

■   What (if anything) happens to the bread and wine of communion? In what sense *are* they the body and blood of Christ?

■   When does it happen? (That is, at what point?)

The basic issue is, what did Jesus mean when he took bread, gave thanks and said, 'This is my body'? Having told us to do the same, what did he think we would achieve by it? Some Christians have understood Jesus' words to mean that the bread and wine change in some sense. They therefore expect the essence of the Eucharist to be the fact that Christ is made present. This naturally leads to a great reverence for the bread and wine themselves. It also explains why, in the Middle Ages, it was enough just to watch and to believe that the Son of God was present on that altar, without also needing to eat the bread and wine. This belief naturally leads to other aspects of ceremonial (bowing, lifting up the bread and wine, ringing bells, etc.) so that people know when the change in the bread and wine has happened.

What happens to the bread and wine?

■   **Transubstantiation** (the Roman Catholic position) is the belief that, though they still look outwardly like bread and wine, the elements are changed inwardly (in substance) to be the body and blood of Christ.

■   **Consubstantiation** (Luther's belief) is the idea that the elements become the body and blood of Christ, but are *also* bread and wine.

■   **Receptionism** (Cranmer's belief) is the idea that the bread and wine don't change at all, but that as we receive them by eating and drinking, we truly receive the body and blood of Christ in a spiritual way. As Cranmer put it, we 'feed on him in our hearts, through faith'.

Though these are complex debates about theology, they have huge implications for the way that the liturgy is celebrated.

Some Christians have expected an objective change in the bread and wine, brought about by the right person (a priest) saying the right words. In the West, those key words were traditionally the account of the Last Supper (especially 'This is my body' and 'This is my blood'). In the East, the key words were later in the prayer, when the priest asks God to send down his Holy Spirit on the bread and wine. Recent liturgical revision in the West has drawn on this Eastern pattern and usually includes in the Eucharistic Prayer a calling down of the Holy Spirit (which is known technically as the 'epiclesis') either on the bread and wine, or on the those who will receive them, or on both.

Both Calvin and Cranmer looked for the believer to be specially united with Christ in the service – though not by Christ coming down to the altar through the consecration of bread and wine, but by the believer being lifted to heaven where Christ dwells at the right hand side of the Father.

More recent thinking has taken the focus off the elements and the words and onto the actions. Not 'bread and wine', but 'eating and drinking' is the key. Jesus, after all, did not command the disciples to '*Say* this in remembrance of me,' but to '*do* this'. Modern eucharistic prayers are constructed on the basis that the whole action of giving thanks is what consecrates the bread and wine (in whatever sense this is understood) and this is not focused on any one set of words in particular. In many churches the charismatic movement has reminded people that the presence of Christ is promised in Scripture primarily through the ministry of the Holy Spirit (John 14.16ff. and 16.12ff.) and that this promise is not limited to the Eucharist. Worshippers have begun again to discover the presence of Christ in all their worship, as well as in the world.

Forget me not

When Jesus told the disciples in the upper room to 'Do this in remembrance of me', he used a Greek word, *anamnesis* (or rather, he would have used an Aramaic word which the Gospel writers translated as *anamnesis*). In English this word gets translated as 'memory', or 'remembrance', or sometimes 'memorial'. All these English words and phrases are about bringing to mind events in the past. *Anamnesis* has a much stronger sense of bringing a past event into the present and making it real for people today. The Jews had a strong sense of this. At the Passover meal they say things like 'we were in slavery in Egypt' – not 'our ancestors were in slavery in Egypt'. We are part of the past event. Much has been made of this aspect of the word *anamnesis* and how the Eucharist can bring into the present the death and resurrection of Christ in a much stronger way than simply 'recalling' the event in our minds.

Some scholars go further. They believe that Jesus was not concerned about what we do in our minds by 'remembering', but about what God does when he 'remembers'. In the Old Testament a cry to God to 'remember' is a cry to God to act (see, for example, Deuteronomy 9.27; Nehemiah 1.8 and 5.19). These scholars suggest that Jesus wanted us to remember him before God, and intended the sharing of bread and wine by his disciples to be an enacted prayer for God to act and bring in the kingdom. In this understanding, doing this in remembrance of Jesus is even less of a backward look to the Last Supper or Jesus' death, and even more a forward look to the expectation of the coming kingdom of God.

Eucharistic checklist

The Apostolic Tradition (a third-century church document, usually ascribed to a bishop called Hippolytus) contains a 'model' eucharistic prayer for use at the ordination of a bishop. What it says later is, 'It is not at all necessary for him to utter the same words as we said . . . but let each pray according to his ability.' We have no idea how typical it was, or how widespread this basic pattern was. However, because it is one of the earliest texts that we have, it has been very influential and much copied in recent liturgical revision, both verbatim and as part of the basic ground plan for a eucharistic prayer.

Most modern eucharistic prayers include the following elements in one form or another:

- an opening dialogue between president and people;
- thanksgiving for various aspects of God's work in his world (often covering the story of creation and redemption);
- the Sanctus ('Holy, holy, holy'), sometimes with the Benedictus ('Blessed is he who comes in the name of the Lord');

- the account of the Last Supper (in some traditions this is not part of the prayer itself but is read before or after it);

- some deliberate statement that we are doing this in remembrance (*anamnesis*) of Christ, as he commanded;

- a prayer for God to use the bread and wine that we may feed on Christ (sometimes, more explicitly, that the bread and wine might become or 'be for us' the body and blood of Christ);

- a prayer for God or the Holy Spirit to come upon us and/or the bread and wine (epiclesis);

- some final praise, and often a look ahead to the heavenly banquet;

- the 'Amen' of the people. Traditionally this has been very important, as a sign that the Eucharist belongs to the people as well as to the priest or minister. The people give their assent by their 'Amen'. In some modern eucharistic prayers the people join in with other responses throughout the prayer, and so the 'Amen' becomes less significant: the ongoing responses show the congregation's crucial role. For instance, Eucharistic Prayer H in the Church of England's *Common Worship* Holy Communion Order One has no 'Amen' at all at the end of the prayer, though the congregation say very significant parts of the prayer itself.

The Lord's Prayer in the Eucharist

The Eucharistic Prayer is usually (but not always) followed by the Lord's Prayer. In this position the Lord's Prayer acts as a link between the Eucharistic Prayer and the distribution of the bread and wine – a form of preparation for receiving communion. It took this position in the Eucharist in both the ancient Eastern and Western streams of the Church, but it is not universal. For instance, in the Church of England in the sixteenth century, Archbishop Thomas Cranmer took the view that the Lord's Prayer fitted more naturally if it *followed* the reception of the bread and wine by the congregation and so he put it in that position in *The Book of Common Prayer*. In addition, he continued the medieval practice of using the Lord's Prayer as a way of beginning the service, so that the service is sandwiched between the two occurrences of the prayer, as if it were itself a practical outworking of all that the prayer encompasses. In other traditions the Lord's Prayer tends to be used as a conclusion for the prayers of intercession, whether the service is a eucharist or not.

Though the 'daily bread' of the Lord's Prayer is most naturally understood as the food that we need day by day, there is a long tradition which links it with the bread of the Eucharist. When our four-year-old daughter used to pretend to distribute Holy Communion in a game at home, she placed the 'bread' (usually a sweet!) in someone's hand and said, 'Your daily bread'. This is not a connection that she had been taught. She had observed the importance of bread in communion. She was also familiar with the reference to bread in the Lord's Prayer, which she knew from our daily family prayers. She very naturally made a connection between the two, and she has not been alone in doing so in church history.

The breaking of the bread

Next we move to the third of the four actions: the breaking of the bread. In theory this ought to be primarily a practical necessity, to make ready for the next key action, the distribution of the bread. Indeed, it is possible to omit it as a separate action and simply to break the bread piece by piece as it is given to each communicant. However, because the act of breaking has come to be seen as symbolically significant (the many parts and the one loaf being symbols of our unity within the body of Christ), it tends to be treated as an action in its own right before the distribution.

Loaves or wafers?

Where a loaf of bread is used there is still a strong sense of the essentially practical nature of this action. There is also a clear symbol of unity, often underlined by the use of the apostle Paul's words:

> *The bread that we break, is it not a sharing in the body of Christ? Because there is one bread, we who are many are one body, for we all partake of the one bread.*

> *1 Corinthians 10.16-17*

This symbolism (and the use of this verse) is completely subverted by the use of individual wafers, which speak most naturally of the exact opposite – of individualism and independence. Their use is often supported on the basis that they are unleavened, like the bread of the Passover – though, as we have already seen, there is uncertainty as to whether the Last Supper was a Passover meal, and ordinary Jewish meals (which seem to have had a strong influence on the development of the Eucharist) used leavened bread. The early Church practice was to use leavened bread, and this continues to be the practice in the Eastern churches. The use of unleavened bread had developed in the West by the eleventh century, when the consecrated bread began to be used for devotional purposes (as a focus for prayer) rather than for consumption at the service by the people. Unleavened bread was good for this because it kept for longer without going mouldy. It had useful biblical warrant in the fact that the Passover was the feast of unleavened bread. Individual wafers were a nineteenth-century invention when the need to 'reserve' the consecrated bread (both for devotions and for taking communion to the sick) was combined with a situation in which the whole congregation received the bread and wine regularly. In this context, a reverence for the consecrated bread meant that it was an advantage to avoid unnecessary crumbs.

In order to make some sense of the symbolism, a large wafer is often used in addition to the individual ones, so that at least something can be broken. There is an intriguing parallel to this in the practice in many Free Churches. Here an ordinary loaf is likely to be used for the bread but individual glasses are provided for the wine. The symbolism of sharing from one cup (1 Corinthians 10.16) is clearly lost. To make up for this, and to echo the Last Supper accounts, there is often one large cup on the table for use during the Eucharistic Prayer, and from which the minister is likely to drink, in addition to the small glasses from which the rest of the people drink.

Both individual wafers and individual cups developed in the nineteenth century at a time when industrialization made their manufacture easy and cheap, and when a new awareness of the importance of hygiene made their introduction easy to recommend.

The words used (if any) to accompany the breaking of the bread vary from church to church. The song Agnus Dei ('Lamb of God') is often said or sung at this stage. It picks up on one line of the song often used earlier in the Eucharist, the Gloria in Excelsis ('Glory to God in the Highest') and acts as an extended meditation on that line. It was originally a much fuller litany of prayer and has not always been associated solely with the breaking of the bread.

The eating and drinking

This is the fourth and final part of the action, in which we finally 'do' what Jesus commanded us. We often think of it as, 'eating and drinking as we remember Jesus', but the Greek implies that we remember Jesus *in the act of* eating and drinking. In other words, this is not a merely cerebral activity, accompanied by a strong visual aid, but 'an action which remembers', and by which we are shaped as believers.

In some churches this involves moving forward to receive the bread and wine. Sometimes this means receiving the bread and wine standing as you reach the head of a queue, where stationary ministers give each person the bread and wine. In the Church of England it has become traditional to come forward to kneel at a communion rail, behind which ministers with the bread and cup move from person to person. In fact there is nothing in modern Church of England orders of service that gives directions about how the bread and wine should be distributed or received. The rails were not originally intended for kneeling at, but to mark out the space round the altar-table (and, some suggest, to keep the dogs away in times when church buildings were not treated with the reverence accorded them today).

In some churches everyone stays in their seats and the bread and wine are passed from person to person. It is a common Methodist custom (also followed in some other Free Churches) to receive 'by tables'. A group of people come forward and sit, kneel or stand around the table while bread is brought to each person. They wait for all to be served and then eat the bread at the same time. The wine is distributed in individual glasses and then consumed by all at the same time in a similar way. A blessing or dismissal is given to those people, who return to their seats, making room for the next group of people to gather round the table.

Like the different names for the service, the different ways and places for eating and drinking symbolize, and form in us, some very basic attitudes and assumptions about God and our lives as

Christians, such as:

- God's holiness and 'otherness', and yet his accessibility;
- our fellowship and equality as we gather round one table;
- the way God takes and uses ordinary things and actions for his purposes.

None of this, of course, is nearly as powerful in shaping our assumptions about God and the Christian faith as the question of who is actually able to do the eating and drinking. We have seen that in the medieval period the answer to the question, 'Who eats the bread and drinks the wine at communion?' was, for most of the year, 'The clergy only'. The restoration of eating and drinking as the central act of the Eucharist was a very significant part of the Reformation's contribution to liturgical change. It gave liturgical 'shape' to their strong belief in the importance of salvation by God's grace, received by faith alone, and to the basic equality of believers at the Lord's table. Interestingly, the same Reformers were often keenest on other 'tests' which would place a restriction on who could receive communion. In many Reformed churches, what we might call 'lifestyle requirements' were imposed, such as the requirement of *The Book of Common Prayer* that no one who is 'a notorious evil liver' should be allowed to come to the Lord's Table until they have shown true repentance.

Other requirements were also imposed. In the thirteenth century the Western Church had determined that no one should receive communion until they had been confirmed. The Reformers now required that before someone could be confirmed they had to know their catechism. This involved giving the answers to a series of basic theological questions and knowing by heart certain texts, such as the Apostles' Creed, the Ten Commandments and the Lord's Prayer. This clearly ruled out young children from being confirmed, and thus from receiving communion. The question about whether very young children are appropriate persons to receive communion persists as a live issue in many churches to this day. Even when the rules change (as they have in some churches in recent decades), the liturgical context (for instance, the words that are used, the mood that is set, the manner in which the bread and wine are made available and shared) will indicate whether children are genuinely expected and valued as communicants.

More radically, some churches have questioned the very basic assumption that baptism is a requirement for the reception of communion, and have adopted a completely 'open table' approach in which any who wish to do so may receive the bread and wine, irrespective of baptism, confirmation or any other criteria. This, too, like every other decision about corporate worship that we have considered in this book, both reflects and creates profound assumptions about the nature of God.

From here to eternity

In these last two chapters we have taken our eyes off the bigger picture and focused instead on particular elements of liturgical worship as it is often experienced. In doing this we have risked being in a position where we cannot see the wood for the trees.

It is important, therefore, to remind ourselves of where we began, which was with the idea that Christian worship is not primarily about what we do when we gather as the Church, but about how we live when we engage with the world, day by day and hour by hour. We have also seen that our imaginations need feeding with the possibilities of the new creation that is yet to be – they need to be given a taste of heaven. Gathering as the body of Christ for corporate worship is a vital part of that feeding and shaping, making us ready for God's coming reign. All corporate worship does that. Believing in liturgy means believing that these things are simply too important and too formative to be allowed to happen by accident.

For further reflection…

1. During which part of a eucharist do you feel that you most 'connect' with what is going on?

2. Have you had the experience of going to a eucharist and not receiving the bread and wine (either because you were not allowed to, or because you chose not to)? How did you feel?

3. Some churches offer a prayer or a blessing to those who do not, or cannot, receive the bread and wine at communion. Do you think this is a good thing or not? Why?

Appendix
Where next? Ideas for further reading

The following does not attempt to provide a thorough bibliography, but does suggest places where the non-specialist might look for readable material to form the next step in following up what they have read here.

General

Paul Bradshaw, *Early Christian Worship: a basic introduction to ideas and practices*, SPCK, 1996 – a slim volume packed with historical information about the early development of liturgy, particularly Christian Initiation, the Eucharist and Liturgical Time.

Paul Bradshaw (ed.), *The New SCM Dictionary of Liturgy and Worship*, SCM Press, 2002 – full of concise and reliable articles about all aspects of liturgy.

Chesleyn Jones, Geoffrey Wainwright, Edward Yarnold and Paul Bradshaw, eds, *The Study of Liturgy*, SPCK, 2nd edition 1992 – a good standard textbook, with chapters on all the major aspects of liturgy and its historical development.

Frank Senn, *Liturgy – Catholic and Evangelical*, Fortress Press, 1997 – a huge, thorough and very readable work from an American Lutheran. Particularly strong on the Reformation liturgies, but an excellent overall history.

1 What is Christian worship?

Christopher Cocksworth, *Holy, Holy, Holy: worshipping the trinitarian God*, Darton, Longman and Todd, 1997 – good coverage of New Testament and early Christian worship, with theological exploration of what it means to believe in and worship a trinitarian God.

David Peterson, *Engaging with God*, Apollos, 1992 – a very thorough look at biblical material that has a bearing on our understanding of worship from a Christian perspective.

2 What is liturgy?

Mark Earey, *Worship as Drama*, Grove Worship Series No. 140, Grove Books, 1997 – a booklet which takes further the connections between drama and corporate worship.

Gordon Lathrop, *Holy Things: a liturgical theology*, Fortress Press, 1993 – a stimulating consideration of what liturgy is and how it forms us as Christians.

John Leach, *Living Liturgy*, Kingsway, 1997 – a humorous, practical and impassioned plea for liturgy and spiritual renewal to be seen as complementary rather than mutually exclusive.

Frank Senn, *New Creation: a liturgical world view*, Fortress Press, 2000 – a consideration of how liturgy forms our world-views, with chapters on 'Liturgy and...' covering God; Christ; Creation; Prayer; Evangelism; Culture; Life; and many more.

3 Where does all this liturgy come from?

Paul Bradshaw, *The Search for the Origins of Christian Worship*, SPCK, 2nd edition 2002 – an excellent guide to how scholars piece together the forms of early Christian worship, with warnings about making assumptions.

John Fenwick and Bryan Spinks, *Worship in Transition: the twentieth century liturgical movement*, T&T Clark, 1995 – an account of the history and principles of the 'Liturgical Movement' and the liturgical revision that it fuelled across the denominations.

Larry Hurtado, *At the Origins of Christian Worship*, Paternoster Press, 1999 – a concise study of the wider social and religious context in which Christian worship first took place.

4 Where does the Eucharist come from?

Paul Bradshaw (ed.), *Companion to Common Worship*, Vol. 1, SPCK, 2001 – Chapter 6 on Holy Communion has a very clear and concise history of the development on the Eucharist.

I. Howard Marshall, *Last Supper and Lord's Supper*, Paternoster Press, 1980 – for a detailed study of the biblical accounts of the Last Supper and the development of the Lord's Supper in the New Testament and early Church.

5 Liturgy and the ordering of time

Paul Bradshaw, *Two Ways of Praying: introducing liturgical spirituality*, SPCK, 1995 – a brief but stimulating guide to the development of Christian prayer, with some suggestions for modern revisions.

George Guiver, *Company of Voices: daily prayer and the people of God*, Canterbury Press, 2nd edition 2001 – a thorough but accessible history of Christian daily prayer.

Michael Perham, *Celebrate the Christian Story*, SPCK, 1997 – a short and very readable guide to the Church of England's *Common Worship* lectionary and calendar.

6 Liturgy and the ordering of the imagination

Anne Dawtry and Christopher Irvine, *Art and Worship*, Alcuin Liturgy Guides, No.2, SPCK/Alcuin, 2002 – an exploration of the interface between the visual arts and worship, with practical advice about works of art in churches.

Richard Giles, *Re-Pitching the Tent: reordering the church building for worship and mission in the new millennium*, Canterbury Press, 2nd edition 1999 – a challenging call to Christians to recover a bold sense of church buildings as centres for mission as well as worship, which should be shaped to reflect what we think we are doing.

Andrew Wilson-Dickson, *A Brief History of Christian Music*, Lion, 2nd edition 1997 – a good starting point for an overview of music and how it has been used in Christian worship.

7 Elements of liturgical worship 1: some basics

Horace T. Allen and Joseph Russell, *On Common Ground: the story of the Revised Common Lectionary*, Canterbury Press, 1998 – a short account of the origins of and principles behind the ecumenical three-year lectionary.

Susan J. White, *Groundwork of Christian Worship*, Epworth Press, 1997 – a good basic introduction to Christian worship, which looks at the elements of worship as well as a historical account of its development.

8 Elements of liturgical worship 2: the Eucharist

Paul Bradshaw (ed.), *Companion to Common Worship*, Vol. 1, SPCK, 2001 – Chapter 6 on Holy Communion includes commentary on each section of the Church of England's *Common Worship* orders of service.

Kenneth Stevenson, *Do This: the shape, style and meaning of the Eucharist*, Canterbury Press, 2002 – an exploration of the action and meaning, as well as the history, of the Eucharist. Also looks in detail at the eight eucharistic prayers of the Church of England's *Common Worship* Holy Communion Order One.

Index